"As the social media world continues on its accelerated trajectory, touching all our lives, *Delivering Effective Social Customer Service* is a book whose time has come. It is a perfect how-to guide for all organizations, whatever stage they are at in adopting social as a route to better servicing their customers, helping companies to identify where they sit on the social continuum.

It is extremely thought-provoking being both a perfect primer for those who are at the start of their journey, as well as having loads of useful ideas and tips for those organizations who have already started using social media channels to enhance their service offering. A truly enlightening read!"
Amy Scott, Managing Director, Sedulous

"This is a book which every business should read. Social customer service is here to stay and the costs of not getting it right are usually not even understood. This topic is one that our members constantly ask about and it is fantastic to see such a clear and concise introduction. This will be of immense help to anyone wanting to learn more. It is a book you will want to read and then keep going back to. Both Martin and Carolyn have concisely distilled an unbelievable breadth of experience."
Paul Smedley, Founder & Chair Professional, Planning Forum

A compelling and important book on the biggest trend in customer care. Written in concise, captivating language and filled with expert insight, best practices and actionable examples. HIGHLY recommended for anyone currently engaged in social customer service or about to embark upon it. If you are a customer service or contact centre supervisor, manager or executive and are thinking about NOT reading this book, I advise you to think again."
Greg Levin, Founder of Off Center

Delivering Effective Social Customer Service is a rare find: for the novice, it offers a compelling introduction to social customer service; for the expert, it provides an essential guide to emerging best practice. Beyond the many

valuable insights and examples, which are expertly explained and dissected, readers are taken on a fascinating journey which deposits them – their mind still buzzing – at a vision of a new type of organization: one with collective goals and One Agenda. I commend Martin and Carolyn on their achievement; few people have such a profound understanding of the social customer psyche.
Luke Brynley-Jones, Founder & CEO, Our Social Times

"Social media is a topic clouded by hyperbole and confusion – the perfect environment for unscrupulous 'gurus' and IT vendors to exploit. So thank goodness for *Delivering Effective Social Customer Service.* Forget the empty platitudes of self-appointed social experts, this is a book by customer service professionals for customer service professionals. Therefore we not only get a concise introduction and overview of the topic, but a comprehensive list of key competencies, quick wins and recommended actions – genuine actionable information.

Also boasting extensive references to guide further investigation into the field, Carolyn and Martin's book should provide an ideal platform for the development of your company's social media customer support strategy and its execution. Highly recommended."
Neil Davey, Editor of MyCustomer.com

"I have friends who feel they can ignore social media. However, business can't afford to have the same attitude towards this channel which influences customer service and brand so directly and publically. This excellent book is a great read for businesses – big and small – who are grappling with how to manage social media in a practical way. It is packed full of information and good advice for those wanting to make the smart moves."
Elizabeth Taylor, Chief Operations Officer, Zurich Australia Insurance Limited

DELIVERING EFFECTIVE SOCIAL CUSTOMER SERVICE

DELIVERING EFFECTIVE SOCIAL CUSTOMER SERVICE

HOW TO REDEFINE THE WAY YOU
MANAGE CUSTOMER EXPERIENCE
AND YOUR CORPORATE REPUTATION

CAROLYN BLUNT

and

MARTIN HILL-WILSON

WILEY

Registered office

John Wiley and Sons Ltd, The Atrium, Southern Gate, Chichester, West Sussex, PO19 8SQ, United Kingdom

For details of our global editorial offices, for customer services and for information about how to apply for permission to reuse the copyright material in this book please see our website at www.wiley.com.

Wiley publishes in a variety of print and electronic formats and by print-on-demand. Some material included with standard print versions of this book may not be included in e-books or in print-on-demand. If this book refers to media such as a CD or DVD that is not included in the version you purchased, you may download this material at http://booksupport.wiley.com. For more information about Wiley products, visit www.wiley.com.

Library of Congress Cataloging-in-Publication Data

A catalogue record for this book is available from the British Library.

ISBN 9781118662670 (hardback)   ISBN 9781118662656 (ebk)   ISBN 9781118770566 (ebk)

Cover design by Andrew Ward

Set in 10/14.5 pt Palatino LT Std by Toppan Best-set Premedia Limited
Printed in Great Britain by TJ International Ltd, Padstow, Cornwall, UK

CONTENTS

FOREWORD

This book is for the people still arriving.

You might have no affinity for Social Customer Service. You might read this as an expert and tell us what we got wrong. The book you are now reading is an exploration of "old world" experience mashed up with "new world" aspiration.

We wrote it to provide another perspective. Both of us come from the world of Customer Service. We get the people from that world. We know the issues. We've moved out of that comfort zone and embraced the mindset of being social. Getting to grips with what that means in a Customer Service context.

So we write about it. We provide courses on it. We listen out and learn as new insight and lessons emerge. We saw a need to bring together the best thinking and examples of Social Customer Service that are spread across the social web and get them organized into something that helps you plan and execute a great service experience. We then filtered that through our collective experience.

This is the result.

This book's trajectory is optimistic. Hopeful that what is currently labelled Social Customer Service will evolve into something much more valuable. Namely that our industry's collective ambition moves on from reactively fixing customer issues which in truth ought to be anticipated and removed from our customers' lives.

We live in new times. Social Customer Service is just the start.

A QUICK INTRODUCTION TO
READING THIS BOOK

If you are a traditional lover of books and just prefer to read cover to cover then please consume the book's ideas in this way. However, if you are intent on flicking through to pick out ideas for immediate use, then here are a few tips.

Chapters 1 and 2 are scene setters that provide an overview of how both customers and organizations have found reason to use social media as channels for interaction. Chapter 3 then moves onto the building blocks of a Social Customer Service ecosystem and begins to tease out some of the issues.

Chapter 4 then changes gear and is a little different. For a start it is much longer. It is the centre of the book in terms of using the ideas and comes in the form of a self-assessment. This is an exploration we very much hope you complete and get value from.

It defines 15 competencies that support your ability to deliver a great Social Customer Service experience. If you are a veteran of Customer Service strategy you will no doubt recognize parts of the discussion. Completing the assessment enables you to design version one of your Social Customer Service strategy.

Chapters 5 to 7 then dig deeper into the character and operational best practice for peer-to-peer support, Facebook and Twitter.

After that we tackle two core topics in Chapters 8 and 9 – crisis management and the relationship between social interaction and the law. Finally, we draw things to a close by considering the "big picture" issues that social engagement throws up. How do organizations need to adapt in this new order? A topic for the top table to consider.

Peppered throughout the book are a series of interviews with some of the most interesting people in the field of Social Customer Service today. These are a great source of practical wisdom and if you like to learn through stories then this will also be a fun way of cherry picking.

As we mentioned in the Foreword, one of our motivations was to consolidate existing material spread across the social web. Any search engine ought to find the full original versions for you. However, we have also made them available on a website dedicated to readers of this book. Log on and you will have access to all the reference material as well as some extra goodies we could not squeeze into the book.

www.socialcustomerservices.com

Who knows – it might even evolve into a social discussion amongst us all. We look forward to the chance of getting to know you personally.

Till then,
Happy reading.
Carolyn and Martin

Chapter 1

Where Were You When It All Changed?

If you are just waking up to Social Customer Service you might well wonder how all this happened. Since the use of social media such as Twitter, Facebook and YouTube exploded into our lives, organizations initially thought they spotted an opportunity to extend their Sales and promotional activity into new channels.

However, their mindset proved out of synch with the times. For sure they could continue brand messaging as before and even extend their broadcast model to include limited customer response in the forms of "likes" and "follows". In fact this has become the standard way in which organizations have so far defined their customer engagement strategies.

But organizations also discovered that the communication agenda is no longer exclusively set by the brand team. As publically shared platforms, social networks allow anyone to voice their ideas. So began the birth of Social Customer Service.

Customers began to post tweets when they were unhappy or had a question about the product or service. Some strongly worded Facebook groups were established against brands and organizations that were giving bad Customer Service. YouTube videos went viral (see our interview with Dave Carroll of United Breaks Guitars fame). But they all had one thing in common. Customers had tried to get their problems resolved through traditional Customer Service channels, but then struggled to get a satisfactory resolution. Social channels provided an outlet.

Frank Eliason, now Director of Global Social Media for Citi, is credited with triggering the first well reported organizational response to this customer trend. As part of the Comcast Customer Service team, he decided to respond to one of the many unresolved customer issues on Twitter. The flood gates were then forever opened.

In the "I Want It Now" world, operating against a backcloth of mainly indifferent but often poor service quality, customers quickly learned to leverage social media and force organizations in step with their needs on their terms. Some organizations have resented this, saying they feel "held to ransom" by customers that use social channels to air gripes. If untrue, then yes, this is frustrating but also the price of operating in today's socially transparent business world. However, many of them proved real. The balance of power has shifted and we as organizations are learning to deal with it.

Other organizations have seen this as opportunity and welcomed the ability to dialogue with customers in this new way. John Lewis, British Gas, LOVEFiLM and other brands swiftly established dedicated Twitter accounts for Customer Service interactions and created skilled teams within the contact centre to respond to and manage these interactions. They used social media to reduce AHT (Average Handling Time), gaining significant financial benefit plus an improved Customer Service reputation.

Organizations such giffgaff, BT and BSkyB have enjoyed even broader benefits using peer-to-peer support communities as part of their social outreach. While retailers such as ASOS, Next and Tesco host busy Facebook pages with plenty of Customer Service issues being discussed in between the latest engagement campaigns.

As we know from mainstream Customer Service, adding new channels might reduce cost. Self service has slowly but surely chipped away at the non-complex end of customer interactions. But more often the real benefit of multi-channel is about giving customers a *choice* about the way in which they want to interact with you.

Some commentators express great confidence that social channels will rapidly make old school Customer Service redundant. We are not so convinced. The demand for one-to-one private communication via voice, email and web chat will continue. In fact they are frequently integral to Social Customer Service delivery as a way of dealing with confidential matters.

The important point about "choice" is that if you make it easy for your customers to do business with you then they will keep doing business with you.

The politics of social transparency

No-one enjoys being criticized in public. Even thick skinned politicians admit that it can hurt. So it is no surprise that organizations react defensively. When things turn from bad to worse and become whipped up into a social media crisis, the fear factor creeps even higher. Rightly so, since it often costs more than reputation when things go wrong, as some of the stories we tell prove.

Yet there is another more hard boiled perspective that says surely if everyone starts to raise their voice, don't they just cancel each other out? After a while no-one notices yet another public bashing. It's noisy and maybe nasty in this new public marketplace, but that's just the way it is. We will not be noticed so let's carry on with business as usual.

Are these folk right or are they unconsciously playing chicken and walking up a motorway the wrong way with their eyes closed? That is one of the great questions posed throughout this book. Ultimately it is for you and your organization to decide where the real level of risk lies. But we return to it in different ways to keep the topic turning over in your mind.

Here is an initial opportunity to reflect on the issue of how dangerous the transparency of social interaction might be and how you can pre-emptively mitigate that risk. This is one way of looking at it.

One of the most powerful reasons to run a tight ship on social media is just how much it tells competitors where you are going wrong. Take supermarkets. Anywhere in the world there are those in the ascendency and those in need of a transformation. Yet within 15 minutes of sifting through a supermarket's Facebook timeline, supply chain issues are revealed in great detail by customers. In many cases they are willing to write paragraphs. We are no experts in retail supply chain but we can imagine what that competitive intelligence could be used for in the hands of a direct competitor.

Thus Social Customer Service has to go hand in hand with rapid continuous improvement. That is to say execs need to immerse themselves in the detail and get fixing before getting skinned by a competitor.

If you want to test this right now before reading anything else, please try. Go and have a detailed look at what customers are saying about your organization or your competitors. Come back in 15 minutes and re-read this paragraph.

What do you think?

The Only Way Is Onwards & Upwards

Jamie McDonald is Customer Experience Director for Carillion plc.

Jamie has led Carillion through the unchartered waters of Social Customer Service since 2010 and his passion for serving customers this way is clear. Jamie advocates that for brands to have success delivering Customer Service online they have to believe in it. Talking from an honest and open perspective,
Jamie shares some lessons learned from the journey to date. Carillion plc, as part of a wide ranging portfolio of services and construction contracts, provide housing maintenance solutions under multiple contracts in the UK public and private sector. They receive and respond to approximately 200 Facebook posts and tweets from customers every day.

What would be your advice to organizations thinking of embarking on Social Customer Service?
If you have millions of people engaging with you it might be different, but for most SMEs the far biggest cost will be the emotional one, and I totally understand why people are uneasy about it, but it is the right thing to do. If you don't, then your customers will anyway. There were some awful Facebook pages that were set up by customers against us in the early days before we had an official presence that have now dwindled as people have flocked to our page where they know they will get a response. If your customers haven't got a place where they can say what they want to say then they will create it.

It's far better to have them doing it on our page where we can see it, solve it and learn from it than not. But as soon as you begin to try and control it and moderate it, they will defect in droves and go somewhere else. Standard responses, deleting posts, inauthentic language and any sense that things aren't improving will send your customers over the edge. Customers sometimes send out random messages assuming there is a company Facebook site, and are surprised when there isn't. There is a realistic demand that companies have a Facebook site and increasingly a Twitter obligation too. If you don't have a Social Customer Service presence you will increasingly fall behind.

What has been one of the hardest things to deal with in your world of Social Customer Service?

We had a "mugging" on Facebook recently where a customer we'd let down managed to mobilize every person she knew on Facebook and within a few hours we had hundreds and hundreds of posts on our page, many more than normal. It was like a collective mugging, a really powerful, co-ordinated "attack". She'd persuaded all her family and friends and friends of friends to join the site, "like us", and then bombard us with posts about her issue. Our first viral activity and it was really painful to be on the receiving end. This was a co-ordinated campaign to get this lady's problem sorted and it worked.

There are some genuine examples of people trying to get the attention of brands and organizations by using Social to their advantage, trying to jump the queue or get what they want.

At Carillion one of our golden rules is you don't get a better level of service just because you use social media. If you escalate your issue to us through a non-standard channel, whether it is a letter to the MD, a complaint to Watchdog or a Facebook post we will capture it differently and acknowledge it differently, since it came through a different channel. But to provide a differentiated resolution to something just because the customer is savvy enough to use Facebook is wrong to us. That is really hard though, as your own human common sense begins to prioritize the channel because it is visible and global.

And surely there are some people who lie, throw tantrums to get their own way are there not? Does Social simply put power into the hands of people who will use it against you?
You will always get some people that clearly have a lot of time to devote to escalating their issue to us. Like a letter to Watchdog, some people will embellish the story, but unless you are a complete fantasist you are unlikely to make it all up. If they do, you soon find out. We've only ever had one or two. There is some work to do investigating things people say but then wouldn't we be doing that anyway, whether the information is coming via letter or telephone? Perhaps people would have to be more motivated to complain in writing over small issues that they might not have complained about before.

To complain in writing or by telephone when you aren't confident can be difficult. I'm quite proud of the fact that we've given a voice to people who perhaps didn't have it before but because they can use Facebook and find it easier to send a short, informal message. We get more complaints than we might have done otherwise, but I'm ok with that. I think one of the big wins is that a group of customers that might not have had a voice now do.

Do people use the ability to escalate issues through social?
We have had customers send InMail to senior executives via LinkedIn and I personally pick up and respond to tweets from @JamieCarillion so that customers know they can access us through Social. I think it is good for customers but it is also good for the teams to see the senior managers monitoring and engaging the customers. I learn so much from the feedback we get from customers via Social.

How do you manage multi-channel Customer Service? What are the biggest challenges in the execution of this approach?
A key learning point has been when people contact us via Facebook and Twitter about the same issue and they compare our

responses across both and if there are any inconsistencies they will highlight that to us too. We have had to think much more about how we co-ordinate the channels and the responses. Matching up different channel contacts for the person at the front line is still quite difficult. If there is a way of a CRM platform being able to work in real-time around different channels and across regulated and non-regulated contacts we haven't found it yet, bearing in mind people can change their Twitter names and mobile phone numbers!

The theoretical efficient model of a "Single Universal queue" doesn't always work well to move between different channels. Social media is a tool you haven't bought, that isn't maintained by you, but customers see that you have gone in to this model so you need to be equipped to handle it; even though there is no easy way to predict volumes! We have found that activity matches our call centre patterns, which was interesting. We had expected it to be the other way around, that people would use Social more in the evenings and at weekends but it hasn't been the case for us. People post and tweet at us in their normal working day when they would have made the phone calls.

Universal skilling is also really hard. The breadth of knowledge you need and the ability to move alternately between writing a letter, writing an email and writing a Facebook post is really challenging. The model we use is Customer Service and Customer Care. Customer Service is high volume, inbound channels, mostly telephony, and the more simplistic transactional stuff. Customer Care manage social media, complaints and customer satisfaction. This latter is lower volume but greater complexity and much more visible. Both need good written English skills but the latter needs the maturity to use the right phraseology in the right channels. Dickensian English doesn't translate well to social media responses! This model works for us and it also provides a career development route for advisors through the contact centre.

There is an argument that providing Social Customer Service could make you look bad and damage your brand. What do you feel about that?

When customers are in distress they will post rants which might make some companies defensive, but you have to move past that and recognize that the customers are simply saying "help me". If there are unofficial sites on Facebook against your brand then it's a warning that you are not doing something right.

Social is only used regularly by about 5% of our customers but it provides us with a real-time snapshot of what the majority might be experiencing, albeit slanted towards the negative. It might be low volume, but it is definitely high impact. It has as much impact on our customer perception, media perception and our contract renewals as the 95%. It also gives me lots of insight into themes and what the hot topics are for our customers. I don't understand how you can be a Customer Services director and not be interested in that.

It's important to remember that social media will primarily be a place for people to post negative comments. If you have an exciting business offering you will probably get more "thank-you" and posts of delight, but when we deal with double glazing, radiators and boilers, a lot of it will be complaints. Some people read our page and use enforced logic that because it is a lot of negative postings we must be terrible. Sometimes we remind them that 12 have complained this week, but we serve 100,000 people.

How has using Social Customer Service been received by your employees?

3 years ago staff were clamouring to be on the "Facebook team" as it was the new exciting bit, now it's just another thing to do at work, I think the novelty has gone already! An unexpected output we've had from the process has been that our front line guys go home and keep an eye on our Facebook and Twitter pages and read all the posts and our responses. They then come in the next day and give us feedback on our responses which has been really helpful in shaping the tonality and authenticity of them.

In the early days there was a bit of defensiveness from our employees, they would see something on the page and think "that's not true!" and start typing a response. This led to terrible situations of online fights between our customers and employees and we learned a lot of painful lessons around the ground rules. We try not to enforce things but we now show people what the rules and guidelines are using examples.

Are you training people specifically in Social Customer Service?

Social media training is not like Data Protection training where there are some legal sanctions. For DP there is training you can do and you can sign to say you've had it and then you can enforce it. Social media training needs to explain why Social Customer Service is a key part of our proposition but there are some key things to do and avoid doing. It's great if employees want to get involved, "like" the site and look at things, that's fine, but we say here are some examples of where people have tried to do things, with very good intentions, but it's been awful so please don't!

What happened?

One of the biggest problems we had was where two customers started debating about us on our page, one attacking us, the other defending us. One of our employees was at home and saw this debate, and "liked" the pro-Carillion response. The angry customer saw the post had been "liked", clicked through, saw that the person worked for us and went bananas. They then claimed they had been bullied online by one of our employees and caused a huge ruckus over that. But there is no enforcement we can do of someone who in their own time, in their home, on their own machine clicks "like" on a post. It is completely untenable, so our reaction is to use this as an example in training now as to why this sort of thing is not a good idea. I think the way we manage our people to use Social and the way we wrap

HR and Legal around Social Customer Service is still very unclear and some more work is needed here.

What specific training can organizations do to maximize their chances of success?

We've trained in "Facebook English" to ensure our responses have an authentic and consistent voice. When our team are responding to a complaint letter they have an agreed code of language for writing responses and the same again for email, but the phraseology, language and style in Social needs to be different. With social responses you need to write as if you are talking to the person. The customer needs to think "this person gets it and I'm not being spun a line here". With complaints it is important to acknowledge the issue and signpost them offline to the formal channels if possible, but if the customer wants to have the full and frank discussion globally then, providing there is no breach of the Data Protection Act and they are not undermining their own security (as some customers are very honest and open with their details a little unwisely), then we get on with it.

An example of the tonality Jamie is referring to:

Customer post: "I am sick of this: I've reported my broken radiator three times now and still nobody has come out, despite several promises. It's freezing cold and I'm thinking of going to stay with my in-laws so you can imagine how desperate I'm getting!"

Carillion response: "Hi Julie. Really sorry that we've let you down here: it must be a nightmare for you and the kids. Send me a PM with your details and I'll get this sorted today. Don't call your mother in law just yet!"

As well as "Facebook English", what other rules do you apply to Social Customer Service?

Another rule is to avoid censorship and moderation of customer messages that could be perceived for our own advantage. If we have to delete a post (due to swearing, data protection, etc) we always re-post, explaining why and re-post as much of the original post as possible, or explain that we notice that they have a problem with xyz but we had to delete the post as it contained a lot of swearing and that's not good for people.

What are your views on the One Agenda idea? Is there a halfway house needed between Sales & Marketing and Customer Services?

> "If you try and use social channels for Sales and Marketing only then good luck."

There is not a chance that social channels can be a good news channel only; customers will use it for what they want to. The internal discussion about Marketing owning the tool and Customer Service went on but Customer Services was agreed because we have a more 24/7 presence and most of the posts are about Customer Service issues. My Marketing Team agree the branding and description of the Facebook page and then my Customer Care team own the day-to-day management. It is mostly a complaint channel but that's what customers need to express. You can put your messages out through Social, all carefully worded and brand aligned, but customers will just tear you apart. It's not authentic. In the same way that writing formal responses, copied and pasted many times, will make customers even angrier and your social strategy will fall apart very quickly. Having a credible message and the tone in which you respond to things is incredibly important.

How else are you using social media?
All of our job vacancies are tweeted out on a dedicated Twitter handle. Gone are the days of advertisements in The Times and Telegraph. We are increasingly using separate Twitter handles for different contracts and for different purposes (Recruitment, Customer Service).

Has Social Customer Service affected your employees outside of the contact centre?

The power of Social has really hit home with our guys out in the field. Recently we picked up on a photo tweet about one our vans which had been posted by a lady who said the van had cut her up on the road. The van was filthy, with some funny but rude words written in the mud and a broken brake light. It was retweeted countless times. Of all our Marketing activity and other good news that week, the story of this van with the Carillion logo covered in mud got far more coverage. How we respond and apologize and move forward is key. Twitter is a powerful tool and very uncontrolled. In this world of social media, the acts of one of our lads in a van can outweigh everything that is done at a corporate level.

Any final thoughts?

You have to believe that what your customers are saying matters. If you go into it because you think you have to, you will get your fingers burned. You can't play with it. As soon as the channel is there, customers take it over. Start small and let it grow naturally, there is no need to advertise it. Have a clear plan about what your engagement model is. Have clear processes. We found that letting it grow through word of mouth meant that the team could find their feet. Their competence and ability has grown alongside the volumes.

Chapter 2

Understanding Social Customer Behaviour

Customers and their use of social networks

"On the business side, people don't take smoke breaks anymore. They take Facebook breaks."

This simple observation captures just how far our daily habits have shifted. We can now gossip with whoever we please regardless of location, not just with co-located work colleagues as we snatch a hurried mid-morning break.

In fact, nearly 70% of our online social interaction is also location independent. It is now conducted on the move via our smartphone or tablet of choice. In fact the rise of social media and mobility is deeply synergistic. Their interplay continues to reinvent how we go about living our daily lives.

This increasing integration of social platforms within mobile operating systems has made it far easier to share our thoughts, requests and criticisms in the moment. Facebook and Twitter are currently deeply embedded into Apple and Windows mobile devices while Google+ is naturally part of the Android experience. The appearance of Facebook Home, providing an always-active, ever-in-motion, Facebook-centric homepage has merged the social and mobile experience ever closer. The net result of all this integration is to have made social networks both more accessible and convenient for us all.

This evolving behaviour in personal social networking is a profoundly important trend to recognize and respond to for every organization that is intent on meeting their customer experience objectives.

We are at one of those points in history when the speed of change is so rapid and widespread that it seems to noticeably change every time we blink. However, the challenge is this: the rate of adoption amongst your own customers is unlikely to be uniform. The implications being you will need to watch, understand and be especially responsive during this great transition in human behaviour.

For instance, the clear cut value that Skype delivers for grandparents wanting to keep up with family news has meant one type of social networking is already fully embraced for a particular generation with a particular need. For them it is now part of daily life and is trusted. Although yet to be commonly offered by organizations as a Customer Service channel to this generation of customers, the potential is clear.

Looking more broadly at global trends, it might seem the transition to social networking is all but complete.

"Social media is the internet: Social media is so ingrained into the modern internet experience that a staggering 90% of all internet users now have an account on at least one social service and 70% of them contributed in the past month."

However, it remains important to examine the detail. Participation levels continue to vary by platform and by region. Whether this is just a snapshot in time and global habits eventually align more closely remains a guess. However, if you are responsible for either a global or regional Customer Service remit, you will already know that customer behaviour is culturally specific. The news here is that use of social channels is no different.

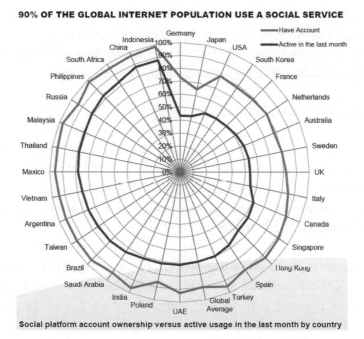

90% OF THE GLOBAL INTERNET POPULATION USE A SOCIAL SERVICE

Social platform account ownership versus active usage in the last month by country

Figure 2.1: Global Web Index Spider
Source: GlobalWebIndex, GWI.7 Q2 2012. Question: On which of the following services have you created an account? Base = Total.

So with that in mind, let's look at some specific data.

This overview of national social networking from Global Web Index (see Figure 2.1) provides us with a couple of important insights.

First we can clearly see that adoption rates vary across the world. Thus the need to keep tracking these over time as part of your planning assumptions is something to note.

The second observation shows a distinction in usage patterns that is important to understand.

The black and grey lines reveal the difference between levels of active and non-active membership within social networks. We are sure you can relate to this on a personal level. Think how many social networks you have signed up for. Since they are free to join, it is pretty simple to sample new services as they arrive. But given time constraints and personal preferences how many of those are you really engaged with?

What can we take from this?

When you hear that Facebook, Google+ or Twitter have just hit a milestone membership number do not assume that percentage of the global village is now fully socially engaged. There is still a personal transition to be made. And some people never make it; maybe not on that particular network, maybe not at all.

Nevertheless, year-on-year growth in the major networks shows that the overall trend continues upwards. Incidentally, this is happening at the expense of national networking platforms which are starting to lose members to their global equivalents.

The next point is that not only are more people continuing to join in, they are also evolving in their online social behaviour:

> "The average number of Pages that a user "Likes" has increased over the past 3 years. According to data from October 2009, users became fans of about 4.5 Facebook Pages. This volume increased to around 30 Pages in the following year, and rose to 36.7 average "Likes" by October 2012."
>
> *Source*: **Social Bakers 10 social marketing facts of 2012**

As we might expect, we become more sophisticated in our use and expectation the more we sign in. And since this is social networking we are talking about, the speed at which those lessons are learned continues to set new records.

Let's now translate these global trends into national behaviour. What do we know about the UK? It is common knowledge that at least half the population have Facebook accounts and according to Twitter 10 million of us are active with them. LinkedIn reports that 4 out of 5 UK professionals are on their network as well.

As a side note, just as we were doing final edits on this section of the book, a report popped into our inbox claiming that "Twitter Now Rivals Facebook As Teen's Preferred Social Network". Why? Who wants their parents knowing what they are up to? In fact the average age of a Facebook user is 40 which incidentally makes it a perfect service platform for many customers.

At the time of writing in 2013, one of the most recent consumer surveys on actual social network use told us this:

- The number of British consumers who have dealt with companies through social media has almost doubled – from 19% in August 2011, to 36% in April 2012.
- Most of them (68%) believe that social media has given them a greater customer voice.
- Most of them (65%) believe social media is a better way to communicate with companies than call centres.

Fishburn Hedges research the "Social Media Customer" (OnePoll Research)

The numbers using social media for Customer Service are somewhere between 10% and 14% during 2012 according to the respective conclusions from eDigitalResearch/IMRG and Amex's Global Customer Service Barometer.

The US experience is even more pronounced – see Figure 2.2.

So what can we learn from this? Obviously, we are now gaining critical mass pretty fast: turning what was a purely personal form of interaction into one increasingly used between organizations and their customers. The issue of scale is not far away.

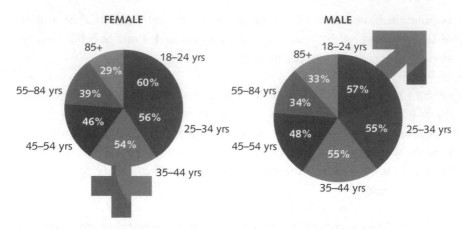

Figure 2.2: US consumer adoption of social networks by gender
Source: Data sourced from NM Incite's 2012 State of Social Customer Service Report.

In spite of this, some brands continue to opt out of allowing customer comment on their Facebook pages. Yet it is now much tougher to restrict the flow of customer commentary. Who owns access to these communication channels is no way as clear cut as an Interactive Voice Response (IVR) or even a web chat facility. Ownership and thus control of social channels is far more evenly balanced. This challenges traditional mindsets over how to become successful in this form of customer interaction.

It also appears that as consumers we are fairly excited about the potential benefits of social channels. Although real world service standards via some social channels suggest this is due to be replaced with a more disappointed and frustrated customer experience; unless radical improvement takes place. Indeed this is one of the reasons that motivated us to write this book!

Here is something else to reflect on. According to some studies, for every complaint that is made more than 25 go unregistered. The vast majority of those then simply take their business elsewhere. This is the invisible fallout from traditional service standards. Since it is hard to see happening, it has been easier to ignore. However, as we heard earlier, customers are feeling more empowered to be vocal on social channels. This raises some interesting dynamics.

- Could the volume of complaints now increase if customers feel more able to communicate? Although that might be "bad" for brand image, it would be "good" for customer retention if that was the result. If this actually starts to happen it will be important for organizations to read the signs carefully before reacting.
- Again assuming this trend towards greater public complaining, brands will need new ways to offset this. Showing they are listening would be a start. Being able to show they are fixing things would be even better.
- Finally, if customers are getting more complaints off their chests, service responsiveness of social channels needs to rapidly evolve.

> "To complain in writing or by telephone when you aren't confident can be difficult. I'm quite proud of the fact that we've given a voice to people who perhaps didn't have it before…because they can use Facebook and find it easier to send a short, informal message."
>
> Jamie McDonald, Carrillion plc

There is one final slice of research commonly put out by the social media monitoring brands that is worth looking at. Given their ability to track social interaction and categorize it by sentiment, a number of reports have appeared that analyze how well a particular sector is doing typically on either Facebook or Twitter.

All the reports reach a common conclusion. It's very tough to come out smelling of roses in relation to service issues – see Figure 2.3. Only the very best organizations have more positive than negative sentiment.

Key findings

Online customer service conversation about the leading 40 brands declined in tone year-on-year.

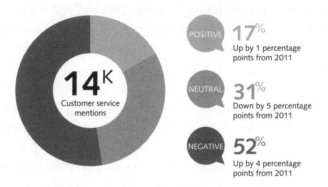

Figure 2.3: Key findings
Source: Reproduced with permission of Brandwatch's Customer Service Index 2012.

They are the names we hear time and again as the best practice service leaders such as John Lewis and Zappos.

In fairness, it should be said that these are snapshot surveys. Another point in time might have produced another set of names that found themselves in credit.

Even so, the underlying trend probably remains true as we can see from the following analysis. The emphasis in the sentiment of customer communications around service issues is more negative than positive.

Again what can we learn from this? First we must get used to an obvious truth. Most service related enquiries coming in via social channels will be weighted towards negative comments. We know this from mainstream Customer Service. However, this time they are out in public view.

We should acknowledge this reality by making it a core planning assumption and consider the implications.

If you intend swimming against the tide then the idea of tying an effective improvement process into your social support workflows makes a lot of sense. You will find us returning to this theme a number of times throughout the book.

Service expectations

Let's now return to looking at specific customer groups and their social networking behaviour since this is where most of our attention will need to be in how we design effective Social Customer Services.

If you group your customers by age there are some interesting points to be made. Younger customer cohorts (16–24-year-olds) have known nothing other than social networks as the major communication platform in their lives. This is therefore their first natural port of call when requiring assistance. As time goes on and their younger siblings become customers, the implications become obvious for traditional Customer Service. This is not to say that those channels will disappear, just that they will need reintroducing into a social network context. We get geekier on this topic during Chapter 4.

Another way to sample customer expectation is by vertical market. Retail provides a rich seam of insight. Certainly within the UK, it is not difficult to find customers asking for updates on their orders up and down a retailer's Facebook timeline. These are nested amongst the more upbeat messages being put out by the Marketing team who are attempting to drive their own engagement agendas. The resulting clash between brand promise and customer experience is something we dig into later in the book when we talk about specific channels.

"Where's my order?" and *"What are you going to do about it?"* is now a spectator sport. Customers growl and brands grovel while others look on. The key question of course is how do those interaction threads influence sentiment?

And while you ponder that let us add one other thought.

Many Marketers are currently being fed the line that "Customer Service is the new Marketing". Of course this assumes that customers' brand perceptions are materially affected by service quality. By the way, some experts do not accept any such correlation. But, if you do see some truth in this headline, then the uphill battle many organizations face in removing recurrent issues from public view by fixing them, suggests this will be a hard won prize. Our own view is that impatient brand owners are about to get a whole lot more radicalized within their own organizations. We shall see.

However, the main point is this: fresh examples of particular segments with particular needs will continue to emerge. It might be based on a generational instinct or it might be driven by a specific market situation. Overall though, use of social channels to interact with organizations continues to grow. Customers also help to cross-pollinate across markets. As use becomes normalized into a customer group's daily behaviour, everyday availability becomes expected.

> "I tweet, so why can't I talk to my doctor like this?"

Maybe by the time you read this you already can.

The lesson here is that organizations need to remain alert to these rapidly evolving customer behaviours and understand when expectations become universal and when they remain niche to a particular segment. What does this mean in terms of planning a Social Customer Service strategy?

For instance, it looks like a reasonable assumption that you will need to resource a social channel mix for your younger customers based on the evidence. This much might be certain. Unfortunately, growth in demand is not as easy as generation based forecasting. The way that socially originated ideas can turn viral, become amplified across other online communities; or popularized through traditional press and broadcast media, means you have to be ready to respond to new demand at short notice.

You may recall this was the instinct of staff being made redundant at UK retailer HMV in January 2012. For 25 minutes the world was treated to a ringside seat for the unfolding drama. Using the hashtag #hmvXFactorFiring, staff were live tweeting (using HMV's official account) from HR, where they were told they were losing their jobs.

Staff or customer, the human response is the same. Of course, this was not the first nor will it be the last time people feel provoked to hit back by going public in this way. It's unfortunate that organizations seem to need these extreme moments before they sit up and change their own behaviour.

Meanwhile, as with all good war stories, we retell them within our own networks – often online. Here is an example found on a financial advisor website.

Tried to have boiler fixed for 5 month and took 5 days to have it replaced thru FBII

- ▮▮▮▮▮▮ , wolverhampton, 18/5/2012
19:38

Report abuse   Click to rate ⇧⇩ Rating ⬆ 1

Certainly tweeting BT has always had much more effect than talking to their painful, formulaic, reading-off-a-flow-chart overseas call centres.

- ▮▮▮▮ , Market Harborough, 17/5/2012
14:32

Report abuse   Click to rate ⇧⇩ Rating ⬆ 4

Quite apart from the steady publicity given to it via this book and the many workshops this example is used in, how fast does this kind of learnt behaviour travel? Are the affected brands even aware they are being discussed on another forum? Probably not.

This is the interesting thing. From a traditional marketing standpoint, getting a brand message to spread across a population is slow and expensive. But we would not bet how long it takes a critical mass of customers to learn new tricks as illustrated here.

Does the customer inevitably win these tussles? Not necessarily. Organizations can and do face down criticism and weather the storm. But it's your call as to whether customers are now gaining some advantage learning ways to fast track service issues on their terms.

Summary

More and more of your customer segments will develop their own reasons for using social channels to communicate with you. Some of that communication will be service related. Somewhere down the line, this "big wheel" transformation will be essentially complete. Bar the digital dissenters, these new behaviours will be fully absorbed by us all.

Of course at this point, if not well before, Social Customer Service will be just Customer Service. Assuming of course that what we currently recognize as Customer Service has not become blended into something altogether different. A topic we shall return to towards the end of the book.

But in terms of thinking about the social networks that have catalyzed this new behaviour, we will let the Global Web Index team have the closing words in this chapter.

Social networks have evolved from mere repositories of personal information where we had a profile and kept in touch with friends. They are, increasingly, woven into the fabric of the internet: built into every webpage, sign on, mobile operating systems and search results. Social networks have evolved to become a set of tools and technologies that link an increasingly multi-platform internet, blurring the lines between our real and digital lives.

The Voice of One Customer in a Digital Age

Dave Carroll is an award-winning Canadian singer and songwriter who reached over 150 million people with his 2009 YouTube music video "United Breaks Guitars". The song chronicled his experience with the Customer Service process at United Airlines and has awakened companies  everywhere to the power of social media as a tool to amplify a customer's voice. Dave is still true to his music roots but now also speaks on the topic of Customer Service and has published a book "United Breaks Guitars".

So, for those that aren't amongst the 150 million people that know your story, what happened?
On March 31, 2008 United Airlines broke my $3,500, 710 Taylor guitar in checked luggage. After more than eight months of unsuccessfully chasing the company for $1,200 compensation, I turned to what I know; songwriting—and I vowed to create a trilogy of YouTube

videos about the incident and I hoped that the first one might attract a million views in one year. It cost about $150 to make and with the help of some friends I recorded a video and put it on You Tube.

Were you prepared for what happened next?
Not really. Four days after its launch, the first million people had already watched "United Breaks Guitars" and it was later named one of the most important videos in Google's history and was in Time's top ten YouTube videos for 2009.

Well it is very catchy and the video is great fun to watch. What was the impact on United?
United stock went down 10%, shedding $180 million in value; I was on CNN and The View. United finally relented and offered $1,200 in flight vouchers and $1,200 compensation which I declined. My promise to make the music videos was not a negotiation tactic. They were my response to their promise to do nothing.

Why did they not just pay you the $1,200 for the guitar repair in the eight months you were communicating with them prior to making the videos?
They gave me a whole list of reasons which just highlight the siloed and convoluted traditional Customer Service process:

- *I didn't report it to the United employees (who weren't present) when we landed late at night in Omaha*
- *I didn't report it in person to the Omaha airport within 24 hours (while I was driving to places that weren't Omaha)*
- *It was an Air Canada issue*
- *Air Canada already denied the claim (but this was because Air Canada would not pay for Uniteds damages).*
- *Someone from United would need to see the damage to a guitar that, over eight months later, was now repaired.*

What is the lesson that other organizations can learn from your story?
I hope organizations are realizing that in our digital world "efficient" but inhuman customer-service policies have an unseen cost. That cost is "brand destruction" by frustrated, creative, and socially connected customers. "United Breaks Guitars" has become a textbook example of the new relationship between companies and their customers, and it has demonstrated the power of one voice in the age of social media.

It has become a benchmark in the Customer Service and music industries, as well as branding and social-media circles. The reason it resonates is that everyone has experienced this frustration at some point or other. I was just lucky enough to be able to put it into a song and sing about it. Before long, I had thousands of people contacting me from all over the world telling me about their experiences and asking me for help.

What was your response to those strangers?
Unfortunately, I couldn't help them all, so with some help from a couple of smart people I set up a Customer Service community called "Gripevine". Gripevine makes it easy for everyone to share their stories in a way that gets companies to listen and take their concerns seriously. It's watched by brands such as Coca-Cola, Mazda, Hewlett-Packard and Cisco and we are well connected with the right people in the organizations people post about. We alert them and when the customer feels satisfied that their "gripe" has been resolved they can change the status to "resolved". The detail of the gripe and its associated resolution doesn't have to be public, which makes it different to posting on social channels like Facebook or Twitter. It is more community based but with some high level alerting from us to the brands.

I'm also working with Resolution1.com to provide a tool for organizations to integrate all social media responses with customer relationship management. Organizations need to be listening before *it goes viral and wipes $180 million off your company's worth. With today's volumes of posts, tweets, increasingly rapidly by the day, there is a need for a tool not just for listening and monitoring, but also for handling the contact, properly engaging and of course, the resolution.*

What would be your advice for organizations to get Customer Service right?

It starts with caring about the people who use your services. You give better Customer Service if you care. I work with senior leaders and people throughout the service chain and we get together to create some bespoke music that really clarifies the values and purpose of their organization. Music gets a message out there in a way people can relate to and remember. I also think resolving the problems before they get out of hand is in your best interest! Social is everything, it has completely and forever changed how we communicate. A random meeting with a taxi driver in Australia convinced me of this; he knew about United Breaks Guitars, he remembered it and he talked about it. The days of companies thinking they can dictate policies and messages to a mass audience are done. Customers are co-creating the brand.

Finally do you still fly with United?

Sure. I'm not going to cut my nose off to spite my face. They have some of the best routes and best prices. United has demonstrated they know how to keep their airline in the forefront of their customer's minds and I expanded upon that satirically. I was angry for quite some time and now, if anything, I should thank United. They've given me a creative outlet that has brought people together from around the world. I think Taylor Guitars were happy too, they had their best year ever in 2011.

Dave's 3 music videos on United Airlines, his book and speaking services are available at www.davecarrollmusic.com

United Breaks Guitars

Written by Dave Carroll (SOCAN)
(c) 2009 Dave Carroll

I flew United Airlines on my way to Nebraska
the plane departed Halifax connecting in Chicago's O'Hare
while on the ground a passenger, said from the seat behind me
"My God they're throwing Guitars out there"

The band and I exchanged a look, best described as terror
at the action on the tarmac and knowing whose projectiles these would be
So before I left Chicago, I alerted three employees
who showed complete indifference towards me

United United
You broke my Taylor Guitar
United United
Some big help you are
You broke it, you should fix it
You're liable just admit it
I should have flown with someone else, or gone by car
cause United Breaks Guitars

When we landed in Nebraska, I confirmed what I'd suspected
my Taylor'd been the victim of a vicious act of malice at O'Hare
so began a year long saga of pass the buck don't ask me
and I'm sorry Sir, your claim can go no where

So to all the airlines people, from New York to New Delhi
including kind Ms. Irlweg who says the final word from them is "No"
I've heard all your excuses and I've chased your wild gooses
and this attitude of yours I say must go

United United
You broke my Taylor Guitar
United United
Some big help you are
You broke it, you should fix it
You're liable just admit it
I should have flown with someone else, or gone by car
cause United Breaks Guitars

Well I won't say that I'll never fly with you again cause maybe
to save the world I probably would, but that won't likely happen
and if it did I wouldn't bring my luggage cause you'd just go and break it
into a thousand pieces just like you broke my heart when United Breaks Guitars

United United
You broke my Taylor Guitar
United United
Some big help you are
You broke it, you should fix it
You're liable just admit it
I should have flown with someone else, or gone by car
cause United Breaks Guitars

Ya United Breaks Guitars
Ya United Breaks Guitars

Chapter 3

The Ecosystem for Social Customer Service

Big picture perspective

Although this book is focused on understanding how organizations can deliver Customer Service over social channels, every so often it is worthwhile raising our eyes to stare at the stars.

The notion of an ecosystem for Social Customer Service encourages us to think more broadly than just Twitter and Facebook. Or whichever social networks are in vogue at the time you are reading this.

In truth, this chapter only manages to skim the surface of what actually lives within this definition. Yet however grand the language of "ecosystems" might seem, it is still only part of an even larger transformation. Let's call it the "digitalization" of our world.

In the work context we already witness the outcomes. More and more of our work activities are available via a browser, on any device, accessible wherever there is connectivity. We can do this on the move, in the air even underground (e.g. the London tube). OK your own organization might be a few beats behind that level of simplified connectivity but that's where the world of business is heading.

In the last decade we have also learned to use this connectivity to be social. We can now reach out as far as we have appetite for being connected to whoever, wherever. Even pets have their own social IDs these days!

However, it is not just the sentient that are enlisting in this digitalization makeover. The so-called "Internet of Things" is putting the objects in our world online. How many will that eventually include? They reckon somewhere between 40–50 billion by 2020! All of them sensing and reporting back what we are doing in real-time.

Add the people, animals and "things" together and it becomes clear why we now exist in a world of Big Data. 90% of the data in the world today has been created in the last two years alone. The projections for its future growth are just staggering. As are the implications for how this changes the way we live.

The reason for mentioning this is that we are only just at the very beginning of how these digital trends interact and open up new doors.

For instance, think about the issue of how all this data can be used. A brand's use of personal data can either deliver an experience of personalization or an invasion of privacy. It all depends on use and context. Equally, customers have unprecedented real-time access to all the variables in a purchasing decision. This makes them at least as smart as those who are selling.

The same disruption applies between government and its citizens, educators and their students, parents and their offspring. In fact any set of relationships you can think of. How this mutual empowerment plays out over the next decade is the context in which we should be thinking about the ecosystem for Social Customer Service.

In other words, this is an ever-evolving interplay that we are describing. It is one that will continue to generate unforeseen customer behaviours, organizational responses and social network derivations.

For instance, at the time of writing video communication is growing. Some say as a reaction to information (text) overload. Equally we are on the cusp of a whole new generation of real-time communication capability (WebRTC). Delivered straight from the browser without a single plug-in. "Click to call" via an organization's Twitter service handle could become the standard way to connect for service and thus usurp the limitations of 140 characters. Who knows?

No-one can forecast the variables that enable a particular trend to prevail. All that can be said is that we live in an incredibly rich world of choice around how we interact and accomplish our daily tasks. It is a transparent and real-time global classroom. As a result, we are changing our communication habits, expectations and assumptions incredibly fast.

Maybe this will slow down when a certain phase of "digitalization" is over. Equally it might accelerate because we have been changed by the experience and therefore relate quite differently between ourselves and with organizations.

One thing is certain. It is now the totality or the ecosystem that drives communication habits. No stakeholder can claim control.

Mapping the territory

So having stared at the stars, what do we do in the short term to make our Social Customer Service work better? First we need to develop a "this year" view of what sits within our Social Customer Service ecosystem. And thereafter regularly update it to keep pace with the changes we just explored.

Of course, if you have the appetite, you can cast your net even wider. Instead scope the task as mapping your "social business ecosystem" or your "multi-channel service ecosystem" if you feel the need for a broader, more holistic context. Ultimately, you will have to join the dots. But you need to start somewhere.

Once you have mapped your ecosystem, it should be broadly similar to other "socially mature" competitors but will nevertheless be unique to your own circumstances.

Why is that?

It's your customers that drive the decision. Where they choose to communicate is ideally what sits within the scope of your ecosystem. Of course the choice is always yours. For instance, do you just want to offer responses via your own preferred channels?

Industry colleagues have cited conversations with senior decision makers who consciously avoid a presence on a certain social network. They don't yet feel ready. Of course that's their choice. Assuming of course they appreciate that ignoring the voice of the social customer is high stakes poker. The first rule in crisis management is that you plan on the basis of "when" not "if". Thus increased warning before your future tsunami is a better risk management strategy.

If this is all too much of a "half empty" argument for you, then here is the "half full" argument. If you already have an appetite for delivering excellent customer experience then this ought to make you sufficiently curious about where your organization is being discussed to include every "watering hole" that your customers visit as part of your ecosystem.

It will be down to your corporate culture as to whether it's pain or gain that finally motivates, but the fact remains your customers' social habits are unique. For sure, they will be on the "big" social networks. But what about the less obvious ones? Your customers use all manner of forums and online resources as part of their online lifestyle. The topic of your organization can be mentioned anywhere.

For that you need a scalable solution for listening. Social media monitoring tools will quickly plot where your brand is mentioned and analyze how this is distributed across what then becomes an initial iteration of your social customer ecosystem. This provides you with an enterprise level of mapping.

As such, it will be of interest to many functional teams. This is the reason, by the way, why your Social Customer Service strategy needs to be consciously aligned with others. Such as your Social Media strategy and your Customer Service strategy to name two of the obvious candidates.

Alignment means making decisions on which "mentions" to respond to, who responds and the overall manner of response in terms of style and Service Level Agreement (SLA). All of it should be planned as a "single version of the truth". So be ready to book a conference room and settle down with your flipcharts for some cross-functional collaboration.

Within that consideration, obviously not all "mentions" are going to be service related. Nor necessarily will they originate from customers for that matter. The ratio of "total" mentions to "service" mentions depends on the market you are in.

Research shows service related topics can be under 1% of all brand mentions or nearly as high as 40%. You need to find out for yourself. Even then snapshot averages don't really tell the story since as we all know it is the outliers that really matter as far as the customer experience is concerned. For instance, a 2012 UK tracking study showed that daily Twitter volumes typically increased tenfold when a "situation" occurred.

So let's pause and consider the implications of what we have just discussed.

Social media monitoring will tell you where your organization is being discussed. Whether those "places" sit in your Social Customer Service ecosystem depends on two decisions.

- Are you/will you operate a cross-functional approach to customer engagement?
- How proactive do you intend to be? Some would argue every mention merits a response. Others decline through limited bandwidth.

The core set of "places" that need to be mapped for Social Customer Service are those from which service related messages are issued. This can range from a specific question on your own Facebook channel to an "in the moment" retweet that provides the opportunity to complain. For instance, an industry colleague used an article headline tweeted by one of us to turn it into a complaint against their mobile provider.

Visualizing the ecosystem

As we have explored, it is easier to recognize demand for traditional Customer Service because the customer has to use the channels on offer which are directly plumbed into the service environment. We then use traffic reports to track and forecast. However, service demand from "social customers" is not nearly as obvious or explicit.

Therefore it helps to visualize where that demand sits and how you intend to build your social channel mix. There is no set way to do this. Indeed most organizations don't do it as such. But it is something we recommend since mapping a territory helps you understand it. This is one way to lay out your map – see Figure 3.1.

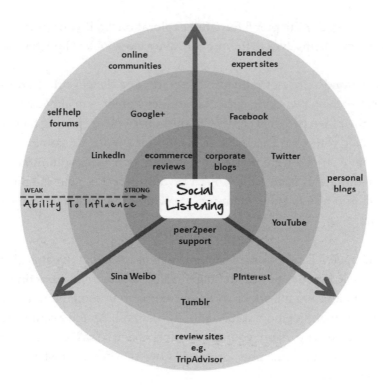

Figure 3.1: Visualizing the ecosystem

Working from the centre outwards, map the social universe in terms of your relative ability to influence. For instance, social interaction built into your own website such as self-help communities are certainly within your influence. You can moderate them, design the look and feel and determine how they are laid out and functionally operate. Of course that does not mean you can entirely control the conversation even though you can set house rules around communication etiquette. But if you mess up big time, still expect the community to let you know in no uncertain terms.

Having a customer community at the heart of your Social Customer Service strategy is hugely desirable. It provides a hub and spoke model becoming a central point of integration. Their benefits are many and the

ROI is strong. See Chapter 5 for a full exploration. So if your product and services lend themselves to this model, take a close look at how they work.

The second "circle of influence" operates at a deeper orbit. These are the large social networking sites that your customers are already familiar with in their own personal context. In this sense you are joining them even if you offer your own Facebook or Twitter facility for Customer Service. Also from a strictly legal perspective you are operating within the terms and conditions of each site: a piece of due diligence that is still often ignored. You also have to communicate within the design parameters of each site.

Nonetheless Facebook brings many benefits. While it remains globally dominant it has the power to shape online behaviour, attracting both consumers and organizations in huge numbers. It is therefore a natural "home" for many demographics although not all. As the average age of Facebook creeps up, many younger members have left in search of parent-free networks. So remember to check how this fits against your own customer base.

As with any Customer Service channel, Twitter also has its strengths and weaknesses. It is peerless as a news breaking platform. This may well explain its popularity with individuals wanting to break their own news about a service issue. But as a medium for case resolution, it's a challenge to say the least. Its 140-character format which even generates its own shorthand to compensate is not for everyone.

It is now common practice to treat these channels as "honeypots" to attract social customers before then systematically transferring them via direct or private messaging to non-social/private channels. As we know from traditional Customer Service, cross-channel is not the same as multi-channel. One maintains the service context while the more common version requires customers to make extra effort and re-explain their situation.

It is a shame so few organizations have mastered this. Bear in mind that some of your social traffic exists because of existing service failure, so you are already on the back foot before adding to customer effort. This is a topic we return to in later chapters.

Nonetheless, organizations can set up dedicated facilities on both Facebook and Twitter to service customers and to that extent influence the service experience. The rapid evolution across all these social platforms also suggests that new functionality can appear unexpectedly as can site redesigns which can make it easier from a service perspective.

For instance, Google's deep involvement with the previously mentioned WebRTC initiative will most likely translate into new Customer Service functionality within Google+. Facebook's introduction of the reply function with conversation threading is a welcome addition. Maybe even Twitter's six-second video service called Vine will prove useful for showing how a product is broken.

You might consider the final "circle of influence" to be "deep space". This is the place where you have little ability to set up your Customer Service store other than to participate in the discussion. These could be forums, blogs or community sites you don't own.

To date, organizations have preferred to maintain a watching brief in these situations. They are content to track conversational trends that might then break out onto the more mainstream networks. Some have been more proactive and directly engaged in discussion. They might feel that facts were being distorted or that a "person in need" deserves outreach even if they might not be directly requesting it.

Research shows this has a mixed impact on customers. When an intervention works and was unexpected, it can have that "wow" factor and therefore become shared within that person's social network. Sometimes organizations get lucky and do that for someone with a celebrity level of followers.

Table 3.1: Attitudes

Attitudes Toward Interacting with Companies Online According to US Internet Users, by Age, Dec 2012
% of respondents in each group

	18–24	25–34	35–44	45–54	55+
Companies should only respond to online comments made directly to them (e.g., on their Facebook page, tweeted to them, etc.)	67.0%	63.8%	63.7%	63.5%	64.8%
Consumers should be able to talk about companies online without that company listening in	40.9%	51.1%	48.6%	49.7%	58.5%
Companies that listen to online conversations are intruding on consumers	40.9%	38.1%	41.2%	41.4%	53.8%
Companies should respond to complaints posted in social media (e.g., Facebook, Twitter)	62.6%	60.1%	58.8%	63.0%	49.4%
If I make a negative remark about a company in an online post, that company should respond to me	47.8%	49.6%	40.8%	53.0%	38.7%
Companies should monitor online conversations to improve products and services	40.0%	53.7%	49.0%	56.9%	36.8%
If I make a positive remark about a company in an online post, that company should respond to me	47.8%	44.4%	40.0%	48.1%	33.2%

Note: top-2 box on a 5-point scale.
Source: NetBase, "Social Listening vs. Digital Privacy, a Consumer Study: Your Practical Guide for How to Engage Consumers Based on Their Attitude Toward Privacy" conducted by J.D. Power & Associates, Feb 13, 2013. Reproduced with permission of J.D. Power & Associates.

However, as customers, we remain contrary. As the research shows, we want to be left alone in privacy when it suits us but also recognized when we need help. Maybe we just want it on our own terms. This is a tricky balance for organizations.

This much is certain. Interventions in "deep space" can either end up as a "wow" or as an invasion. So give extra consideration before venturing this far in your proactive engagement agenda.

Operational considerations

As previously mentioned, one of the issues in participating on a platform owned by someone else is that you operate to their rules and roadmap innovations. The following Facebook example highlights the issue although the implications apply to any social network platform you choose to service your customer on.

"Private messages" was introduced in 2012. "Threaded conversations" was introduced in 2013.

Private messaging has been well received and is a very useful feature for Customer Service. This is because both customers and organizations have the opportunity to withdraw from the public gaze and discuss matters privately. This has obvious uses when confidential customer information needs exchanging. No issues with this innovation.

However, introducing a new feature can have unforeseen consequences for your service capabilities. For instance, at the time of writing, Facebook was just introducing a new set of features. The first was a reply feature. This allows Facebook users and page administrators to directly interact with individual comments within a stream of interaction. It then visually organizes all replies to a comment as a threaded conversation.

This is standard practice elsewhere in most forum style communities. No surprise then that pretty much everyone agreed this made it easier to interact directly with individual readers and keep relevant conversations connected. The only complaint was that the threading only went one level deep. Nonetheless, this clearly benefits a service team's ability to effectively engage by making their responses more targeted.

The second feature was more controversial. It enabled the most active and engaged conversations within a series of comments to be reprioritized directly under the original post. Why was this done? This was the way that Facebook positioned the logic.

> "Also, the most active and engaging conversations among your readers will be surfaced at the top of your posts ensuring that people who visit your Page will see the best conversations."
>
> Vadim Lavrusik – Journalism Program Manager, Facebook, from "Improving Conversations on Facebook with Replies", www.facebook.com, 25th March 2013

At first glance it looked like a value add feature. However, page administrators quickly waded in complaining that in practice this destroyed the flow of conversation and turned it into a jigsaw. Without any option to revert to a chronological order, it appeared to be a regressive step. The impact on Customer Service was also unclear. Might it just point a spotlight on heated exchanges? Or confuse the customer in terms of the history of their interaction? On the other hand, maybe it would help bring priority issues to the service team's attention?

Whatever the final verdict, it was positioned as a new compulsory feature and so organizations would have to live with it. Maybe by the time you read this, Facebook will have modified their position and made it an optional view. But it shows how arbitrary your control on certain core functionality can be at times when under the influence of much broader agendas.

As previously observed, these comments apply in equal measure to any of the public social networks that you choose as a Customer Service platform.

Customer data

The value and role of customer data in delivering effective Customer Service depends on the market you are in and your organization's approach to Customer Relationship Management (CRM). This applies as much to social channels as any other. Whether or not you have traditionally collected interaction history or used customer profiles to customize an interaction, there is a clear momentum towards its use. There are many interlocking trends persuading organizations to up their game in this area.

- The drive for improved customer experience
- The increasing competency to extract value from "Big Data"
- The drive to differentiate through personalization
- Real-time use of data
- The recognition that excellent service is about anticipating the customer situation.

What does this mean in practice? Let's think through a few scenarios.

Some experts are strong advocates of using a person's number of Twitter followers or an influence score such as Klout or Peer Index to recognize "important" customers.

While there are different schools of thought around the value of this type of metric and the notion of treating some better than others, there is also a case to be made around having the ability to recognize your own most valued customers (however, you define that). To that extent being able to pull up the relevant profile data becomes important.

Here is another situation. If I use a social channel such as Twitter on a regular basis for service issues, should I expect to be recognized over time and my needs anticipated given the interaction history that should/ could have been collected? Assuming you are on board with this line of thinking, there are a few issues you need to be aware of as far as Social Customer Service is concerned.

The first point is this. Be clear what the law says in the territories you operate in as far as the use of socially derived customer data is concerned.

This is a fast moving and complex field which is both regionally and nationally legislated. Know where you stand and make sure you set yourself up to remain updated with expert opinion.

Once you have checked that you can use socially derived data, then here comes the next point which is all about integration. How do you match up the way your customers conventionally describe themselves (assuming this is already collected in your CRM system) and the way they might describe themselves online?

Luckily, Facebook and Google+ insist people use real names as a condition of participation in their networks. Equally it would be strange to go by an alias on LinkedIn. However, forums and Twitter are not so easy. In some cases an associated profile of the person will reveal who they are, sometimes not. The question therefore is whether it is worth the time and effort to try and collect this and then merge it with any existing CRM profiles.

Your options to do this are conditioned by the choices you have made around your workflow tool for Social Customer Service and its relationship with your existing CRM system. In some cases it is pre-integrated as in the case of Radian6 and Salesforce CRM, so adding social profile data to existing records is pretty seamless.

In other cases, the workflow tool has its own interaction database that does offer the benefit of showing social interactions over time. If you run Social Customer Service as a separate entity, this can be an attractive option. However, if you accept that the end game has to be an integrated approach to customer engagement, then you will want that data to end up in the enterprise CRM.

This is now increasingly recognized by both the social monitoring vendors who have added workflow to their original competency and the few dedicated workflow vendors in the Social Customer Service space. You will now have access to their pre-built Application Programming

Interfaces (APIs). These allow you to automate the transfer of the customer social data into major CRM system such as Salesforce CRM and Microsoft Dynamics. However, do check that the right APIs are available for your own system. Some of the tier two CRM vendors are yet to have APIs built.

Finally at the least sophisticated end of the market, there are workflow tools that only offer manual export via spreadsheet format. This will suit those on much smaller budgets and those who have no long-term interest in collecting this type of data.

Summary Action List

1. As a cross-functional team, write your research brief to map where your organization is being discussed. In addition to this organizational view, identify the origin, volume and nature of service related topics.
2. Select possible research partners. These could be your existing listening platform provider or one that provides bespoke research. Expect to use their analysts to help you build the mapping queries.
3. Use the mapping exercise to decide on your engagement policy – which topics to track, when to intervene and who then engages on which topics. This will need to be aligned with your "crisis management" policy, social media policy and existing Customer Service strategy.
4. As part of the "who engages" discussion, define your resourcing strategy. This can include full-time service teams, part-time SMEs or customers.
5. Decide if you going to have a community centred strategy or not. This should be based on whether you have a compelling reason for customers to need one.
6. Develop your customer data policy around collection, storage and use. Research the relevant legislation before everything else.

On a Mission to Re-invent an Industry

Joshua March is the co-founder and CEO of Conversocial.

Conversocial's Social Customer Service software is used by companies including Sephora, Groupon, Hertz, Tesco, Net-a-Porter, Waitrose, M&S and more to help them manage the fast growing flow of Customer Service enquiries they are receiving on Facebook and Twitter.

What do you see in the future for Social Customer Service?
I see social growing to be one of the primary communication channels. Over the next 2–3 years the volume of communication will reach, if not overtake, email. This will be a combination of general engagement communication as well as Customer Service. At which point, social team sizes in call centres will need to increase dramatically. Some of our clients currently have got 300 or 400 advisors working on email and their social advisor team is about 30–40 people. I think this will rebalance. In crisis situations, social is the most dominant channel already. As soon as an organization notices an issue you can bet that 30 minutes later it has blown up on their Facebook page.

Why is it growing in popularity so fast?
With the rise of smart phones, it's so much easier and convenient for customers to interact with brands and organizations. It's easier to connect on the Facebook page or tweet from smartphones than to log a call. Some of our major clients are seeing 80% of all their tweets being Customer Service related.

How can organizations prepare for this future?
As the volume of social gets bigger and bigger, advisors need good training, so they can speak to customers publicly on behalf of

the brand. Social Customer Service teams are becoming the public face of the company, for softer marketing engagement as well as Customer Service. It's not just Customer Service; it's also about customer engagement.

The skills required to work in Customer Service are increasing. If your advisors are going be the face of the brand they need to have good written communication skills as well as all the usual people skills.

What's the benefit of embracing Social Customer Service?

Social is a great barometer for CEOs to understand what people are thinking and feeling about their brand or organization in real-time. It provides information that perhaps they should have been listening to before, but it has been coming through the call centre in the form of dry reports for the last decade. Now this information is so much more public and can have much more of an impact on their brand, which is making them stand up and listen.

Social also drives improvements in Customer Service. By making it public and a much more fundamental part of the brand, social is forcing organizations to take Customer Service even more seriously. It's forcing them to solve a problem in half an hour on Twitter which may have taken days over the phone.

How do you get SMEs to engage?

Gartner reports that social advisors can deal with 4–8 times the number of interactions than telephone advisors. The ROI in terms of call deflection and efficiency is big.

However, most brands and organizations using social for Customer Service got started as a result of some sort of crisis. This drives them to get involved. But why wait until you've already had a disaster? The expectation on companies is that they do have a Facebook page and Twitter account to talk to their customers with. 75% of all social media crises were preventable, not in terms of what the company needed to differently but the way in which it was handled online.

Finally, if you don't respond, you are going to lose customers. Tweets and posts are often a last ditch attempt for customers to get a problem solved. Without it they will just give up and go elsewhere. It's becoming more prevalent every day, and if you don't get involved your competitors will.

What advice have you got for companies in a crisis?
Get the CEO/Board in a room with the communications and social teams to craft a fast response, allowing the social team to start engaging and responding with customers 1-on-1. Get hourly reports back from the social team back to Comms and the board. Get the responses flowing through that feedback loop. Interact with your customers honestly and non-defensively. If you argue then it gets worse. Help your customers. Don't go silent. Deal with it head-on, explain what you are doing. This nips it in the bud and prevents it being a bigger issue. If you deal with it properly online your critics will become your advocates: people value honesty, and when you engage with them they are more likely to stand up and defend your company.

Companies that ignore this are putting themselves at much greater risk. Every single day the expectation of consumers goes up and up. In 6 months' time if you start your learning curve doing it badly, you are going to get in so much more trouble than you might at the moment. If there is crisis the Head of Marketing or Head of Social might get fired. I know that's scary, but it is starting to be recognized the effect on the share price that social can have. It's the major factor to drive people to do this properly.

What do you think is the best way to set up social in a contact centre?
For small business and B2B you only need a small number of well-trained advisors that can deal with social as part of their normal workflow. The volume probably doesn't require a separate tool set or separate social teams.

For larger volumes it starts to change, especially if you have large call centres with hundreds of advisors. Tweets or Facebook comments are a public response from the brand that could be picked up by a journalist or retweeted. The only way to work social into this is to have a separate dedicated team. An average full time social advisor can deal with between 500–2,000 messages a month, depending on the complexity of the work. At this point it makes sense to split out for a dedicated team. Not every tweet and message you get will be a Customer Service issue though. We do find that advisors are more productive if they can focus on social purely and again just on either Facebook or Twitter. The mind sets and skills are different for each.

Take your top advisors from the call centre and train them in social. These are the guys that would normally deal with VIPs and they are well equipped to take on social."

What is your opinion on the "One Agenda" idea of joining up social between Sales & Marketing with Customer Services?
In 2012 that used to be a big issue. Now Social Customer Service is becoming so much more important, the volumes are getting so big that Marketing doesn't want to be sitting there answering all the Customer Service questions. Interestingly, Marketing is now trying to give that responsibility to Customer Services and they don't always want it! The response from many Customer Service areas is "why should I do it when I'm getting targeted on call satisfaction and you are getting targeted on social?

From CEO level down you need people to believe in it and commit the resources and force the different departments to work together.

What do you think about fitting Social Customer Service into traditional Customer Service? Does social sit as another channel alongside traditional channels or is it different and separate?
It's another channel but it covers a whole range of communication, so it requires its own treatment, training and processes – and a separate team. However, you still want to integrate data across the

channels, e.g. if someone tweets and then phones you need to be able to see the full conversation across both.

Does that exist yet?

The main challenge is matching up the data. Even if you take social out of the picture companies struggle to match customers across email and phone; customers will have multiple email addresses and multiple phone numbers. The social ID could fix this in future. In 5 years' time, almost everyone will have the same Facebook ID, the same Twitter handle, your credit card numbers, your mobile number all goes into confirming your Facebook identity and while you might change your email, your phone numbers, your physical address, your Facebook ID is probably going to remain exactly the same. Social will be the most important identifier as to who your customers are.

Is Net Promotor Score (NPS) still important?

People find that their customer satisfaction scores increase when they do social well. People try lots of different things to get senior management on board with social. Increasing NPS by 2% isn't it. Being in real danger of a massive crisis is the only thing that really drives people to get on the social bandwagon. Social NPS and effective customer satisfaction only really come into play once the social team is in place and up and running. The only really successful driver I've seen is the fear.

But you still think that once companies are up and running they should be paying attention to NPS?

Absolutely, it is massively important to measure how customer satisfaction changes in social – your most vocally negative customers are exactly the same people who when they are happy will be public about that too. We see that time and time again. And going through rigorous Customer Service processes in social is still important. Data such as how many customers are they helping and what are those customers worth gives the simplest and clearest view of Social ROI. Compare this to how many calls you get and it might seem relatively small in terms of call deflection but it has to start somewhere and it will grow.

What are your top tips for best practice?
It's really straightforward. Ensure that advisors are trained in tone of voice and how to deal with issues. Anything that can potentially result in a crisis needs to be flagged and dealt with properly. Work out what to do with a standard complaint versus an unusual one. Accept and apologize. Look into it. Don't say "we are following legal regulations" or "we are within legal guidelines" online, you will just get people's backs up. Get the tone right from Day 1. Don't delete posts. Don't be rude to people! Don't try to silence critics. Provide speedy responses, you can't spend a week formulating the perfect statement!

Find a way to communicate that matches your brand and customer voice; translate that knowledge into a Social Customer Service team. Marketing have built that knowledge up over a number of years about your customers, find it and turn this into a tone that matches them.

Chapter 4

The Roadmap for Social Customer Service

A s with any new competency, it is probably wise not to jump in head first. Instead do a little homework and get organized with a roadmap. We suggest Social Customer Service is no exception.

The purpose of this chapter is to provide you with a framework and sufficient ideas to produce an initial roadmap. This will provide you with a central plank in your overall strategy. In fact, you may find this is all you need to get up and running. As we said at the start, this is the centre of the book in terms of applying the ideas.

The way we are going to deliver this framework is via a self-assessment of the key competencies involved in delivering effective Social Customer Service. Just how high has the bar been set? Well, we have assumed that by virtue of investing your time reading this book, you are motivated to do the best you can. If indeed that is the case, then this self-assessment will not disappoint! It sets you on a trajectory to become truly excellent.

An overview of the self-assessment is provided below. A digital version is also available on request from us if you need one.

Each competency is fully explored so that its importance becomes clear and any associated issues are mapped out for you. The consequences of adoption/non adoption are also laid out, so you can take stock of each competency's relative importance. There is also a quick wins version. Please note that this is to enable you to map some near term activity on your roadmap. Make sure you still plan for a "full" version. Finally, there is a "next actions" list to take your brain from planning mode into doing mode and put something into your dairy.

There are 15 competencies to work through in all. Hopefully each one will get you thinking. After due reflection, you should complete the self-assessment in the following way:

1. Rate your current capability in that competency
2. Assess its perceived level of importance to your organization
3. Decide where it sits in the timeline of your roadmap.

The scoring mechanism and precise definitions are provided underneath the self-assessment below. Just be mindful about how you approach the business of allocating scores. They are a useful way of completing your exploration of each competency. They will also provide an overview from which you can more easily develop a roadmap and plan. But remember, the real value lies in the thought and debate that precede each score. There is no right and wrong here just best judgement.

You can tackle the job of completing the self-assessment in a number of ways. Either by yourself or as a facilitated team exercise if you are feeling more ambitious and want to build in early alignment. Good luck!

Table 4.1: Social Customer Service self-assessment

	Social Customer Service Competencies	A	B	C
01	We have a Social Customer Service strategy that fits into a broader service strategy and social media strategy			
02	We have the right leadership and development model that optimises our impact in Social Customer Service			
03	We have an effective way of listening to social mentions of our brand and can accurately categorise those that need a response			
04	The level of integration between social and traditional customer service infrastructure supports effective operational management and our intended customer experience			
05	We know how to recruit, train and manage Social Customer Service teams			
06	We have aligned our Social Customer Service competencies with traditional ones e.g. culture, induction, colleague profile, management, policy, infrastructure, SLAs etc			
07	We have identified our platform & the channel mix for Social Customer Service that works for the customer market(s) we operate in			
08	We have clearly mapped customer journeys for Social Customer Service based on their priorities			
09	We are using socially sourced knowledge effectively and have access to relevant customer service knowledge			
10	We are able to build and access social interaction history as needed			
11	We are ready for unexpected volumes of "social" traffic: resourcing, escalation, house style			
12	We have the right balance of metrics that reflect both the customers' priorities and those of operational management			
13	Our SLAs for serving customers via social channels outperform competition			
14	We have a sufficiently detailed understanding from customer feedback to know what does and does not work about our social channels			
15	We are able to learn from social interactions and track improvements			
	Average Scores			

Column A: *Please rate your current capability in this competency*
1 = Very Poor **2** = Poor **3** = Average **4** = Good **5** = Very Good
Column B: *Please rate the importance of this competency for your next generation strategy*
1 = Irrelevant **2** = Unknown Importance **3** = Emerging Importance **4** = Established Importance **5** = Vitally Important
Column C: *Please rate the urgency of operationalising this competency on your roadmap*
1 = Eighteen Months **2** = Twelve Months **3** = Nine Months **4** = Six Months **5** = Three Months

1 We have a Social Customer Service strategy that fits into a broader service strategy and social media strategy

Importance

The process of consciously thinking through issues, clarifying objectives and then prioritizing the things that matter is why strategy is worthwhile, even as a stand-alone activity. You should end up executing more effectively as a result. However, this is not just about developing an isolated strategy around Social Customer Service. Alignment is even more important.

Since strategy often starts out as the creative output of a single team, it needs to become aligned with other relevant ones, so that together they create organizational momentum rather than friction. This is especially important in the context of social interaction since any blind spots generated by functional planning become very evident. So ask yourself how does our social customer strategy fit in?

Consequences

If ignored, the risks include duplication of effort, contradictory policies and disconnection between teams that ought to be better informed about each other's plans. If undertaken, the benefits include more people operating from a "bigger picture", collaboration instead of competition and more agile execution across complementary plans.

Issues

- Many organizations will claim these days that they don't "do" strategy. Don't be put off. Strategy is a design process not a document. Simply invent an approach to considering the issues and documenting the outputs in a way they accept.

- Finding other relevant strategies might not easy. Keep asking. They could exist on paper/in the heads of Customer Experience teams, Social Media teams, and Customer Service or Marketing teams.

Quick wins version

Develop your own six-month "quick sprint" version of a Social Customer Service strategy. This will allow you to gain operational experience before doing the alignment rounds. Aim to do just a few things really well.

Follow up actions

1. Prioritize from all the "follow up actions" in this chapter to produce a "quick sprint" version.
2. Set up alignment session(s) having first discovered if any of the following exist. Then develop an integrated version of all related strategies:
   - Customer service/customer experience strategy
   - Social media/social business strategy.
3. The output of those sessions are customized visuals that show how the integrated strategy links to relevant stakeholders such as execs, customer facing teams, back office teams, external partners.
4. Also produce a project level version that allows you to keep track of all the interdependencies.
5. Share progress on each strategy's roadmap to facilitate swapping best practices, reducing duplication of effort and co-ordinating campaign level initiatives.
6. Plan when to drop the language of "Social Customer Service" as part of normalizing and integrating it into BAU (business as usual).

Tips

Here is a list of topics you might want to cover in your Social Customer Service strategy. This is not intended as a complete list. Invent your own as well.

- Capabilities – culture and skills
- Listening – scope and technology
- Integration – infrastructure and workflow
- Engagement – policies and guidelines
- Ownership – internal and external
- Escalation – BAU and crisis
- SLAs (service level agreements) – social versus mainstream
- Collaboration – internal and external
- Data – knowledge and social graph
- Improvement – method and metrics.

2 We have the right leadership and development model that optimizes our impact in Social Customer Service

Importance

Views about Social Customer Service range from "it's just another set of channels that need integrating" to "this is part of an ongoing business wide transformation in how we engage with customers". Where you and your organization sit in that debate will determine your views on how the service is best developed and led. Over time your response may change as the overall market evolves. Therefore maintaining a certain level of internal debate remains important.

Consequences

If your customers are hoping for a faster, easier, more effective service experience than via existing channels, then invest in a style of leadership and method of "root cause" problem solving that achieves this. This might mean improving existing channels as your first priority. Either way, your solution will need to challenge the status quo. Of course this assumes you intend to improve the quality of service and can win commercial justification for doing so.

On the other hand, if you intend to make your social channel experience equivalent to what you currently deliver, then your existing leadership and development models are the ones to adopt. The reasons for this approach could include:

- You are already meeting customer expectation across all channels including social so service failure is not motivating customers to use social interaction.
- A gap does exist. However, there is no corporate will to fund improvements.

- Ownership of the Social Customer Service team remains in the "wrong hands" for whatever reasons and so the "right" evolutionary path cannot be set.

Issues

- Driving the debate around ownership of Social Customer Service to the "best outcome" does matter to future success. So don't flunk the discussion or settle for a version that is not working. Marketing and PR have their strengths as do Customer Services. Some even conclude involving both is the way forward!
- Functional mindsets and plans often cause downstream issues. Consider the dilution of brand messages when they become nested between publically voiced service complaints. This is most visible on Facebook timelines. How that influences brand perceptions needs constant vigilance and probably a commitment to root cause resolution if proved to be damaging. The outstanding issue though is how Marketing and Service traditionally run separate agendas. This is a prime example of where the right approach to leadership and development needs to make a difference.

Quick wins version

Find a few examples of organizations that already deliver a style of Social Customer Service you admire and believe is what your organization needs. Engage with the people who are making it happen and find out how they squared the circle.

Follow up actions

1. Clarify with colleagues if you intend Social Customer Service to disrupt. If so recruit the right person/team to make it happen. If the current standards work, fold the operation into current structures immediately.

2. Keep reviewing how other organizations are performing. Check out their social channels. If you are a customer try using them. If they impress maybe book a visit to directly see them in action. Keep looking out for what you might have missed in assessing your own organization.

Tips

- Research shows there are four common deployment options to choose from:
  - Centralized within the contact centre
  - De-centralized outside the contact centre
  - A combination of both centralized and decentralized
  - Run externally by a third party e.g. outsourcer, marketing agency.
- If you believe that the transparency of social interaction means Customer Service now becomes a positive/negative driver of brand equity, pay particular attention to the need for:
  - Co-ordinated management
  - Common access to social media monitoring
  - Cross-functional workflow
  - Clear engagement policies between the involved teams.

3 We have an effective way of listening for relevant communication and can accurately identify those who need a service related response

Importance

Traditional forms of service delivery assumed customers always talked to the organization via prescribed communication channels. The so-called "social customer" can still do this by posting on a recognized support channel. But they can just as well be talking about your organization anywhere online. Both approaches need an organization's attention and ability to recognize when intervention is needed. Thus part of the ecosystem for Social Customer Service is the listening or monitoring platform.

This is probably a shared resource, originally selected for its ability to meet Marketing and PR needs. Now it also needs to meet the specific needs of a service operation. Not every platform is capable of satisfying this range of functional demands. Therefore service leadership need to understand what "good" looks like.

Consequences

If your listening process cannot eventually be "tuned" to Social Customer Service needs, your levels of responsiveness remain low. This will become progressively worse if social service traffic grows to rival mainstream channels. On the upside, if you achieve an effective listening capability that includes the ability to moderate and route to "best" resources (the workflow), then bar any outstanding skill and availability issues, you have the means to deliver.

Issues

- Remember that the output of social media monitoring is only as good as the brief you set. So be precise in defining what you are looking for. Both in terms of search capability and overall functionality.

- An engagement policy (when to interact) has to be developed as part of the scoping exercise for the monitoring platform. So an early cross-functional consensus is needed. The scope will include all mentions of your organization – its products, services, activities, prominent staff or ambassadors, adverts and marketing promotions – of which service related ones are a proportion.
- The use of social media monitoring for Customer Service is less developed than for other functions. Many of the more sophisticated monitoring platforms were originally designed for research purposes and, as a result, lack the engagement and team-working features that effective service requires. If you are using an existing solution then make sure you understand its original remit and scope.
- Think beyond the monitoring solution. Consider the whole ecosystem you are building. Does the monitoring solution need to provide your moderated workflow i.e. your ability to assess and distribute posts? Or is that functionality being provided via a third party solution or upgraded contact centre functionality? If used as a workflow tool, is it fit for purpose in a service context?
- Find out enough about how the solution works "under the bonnet" to make an assessment on its overall suitability. For instance:
  - Is the real level of customer demand being missed because the chosen solution does not analyze the right data sources? This links back to knowing where your customers are talking about you online.
  - Which data sources are being used? If inadequate can the required ones (for Customer Service) be plugged into the monitoring solution?
  - How close to real-time are they able to tap into these data sources? For instance not all solutions pay Twitter to have the full "fire hose" i.e. real-time access. This particularly matters during crisis management.
  - How fine-tuned can the queries be built, so that you can find the "needle in the haystack"?
  - Can the solution be integrated with any existing/proposed Customer Service analytic solutions (workflow, tools, reporting).
- The "trick" in social media monitoring, as in all forms of analytics, is to optimize the use of automated search in combination with human

filtering and interpretation. For instance, experts consider the current generation of sentiment analytics (categorizing the positive/negative tone in a post) to be less than 50% accurate. This will have resourcing implications if social traffic grows faster than automation improves. So how broad do you really want to set your engagement policy?

- Don't become over reliant on "sentiment" to find relevant service issues amongst all other social traffic. Remember keyword filters and human moderation are still very much required.
- In cases of existing policy and platforms, the engagement criteria for Customer Service topics might need verifying by SMEs (subject matter experts).
- A plausible reason why organizations have been traditionally unresponsive on social channels is that service related topics are estimated between 1–40% of overall volumes depending on an organization's line of business. In other words they can be hard to spot. This provides a key criterion for what "fit for purpose" means.
- If you are adopting instead of adapting, be aware that currently there are hundreds of competing solutions in the market. Expect ongoing market consolidation. Meanwhile, rely on use cases and industry networking to find and shortlist suitable solutions

Quick wins version

Use your contact centre front line teams to build detailed descriptions of the issues and keywords they are repeatedly exposed to as a way to develop your initial monitoring brief.

Follow up actions

1. Gather together platform stakeholders to debate and agree your engagement policy (when to interact). This then informs how the listening platform is used. Each function (Marketing, Sales, PR, Customer Service etc.) needs to decide when and why to respond. This should be done in reference to strategic aims (question 1).

2. Meet with internal users of any current social monitoring solution and find out what it can and cannot do. Likely candidates are Marketing or Communications.
3. Develop your Customer Service brief and "fit for purpose" questions. Use contact centre front line to source topics. Meet with the vendors (existing or new).
4. Go see what other equivalent organizations use.
5. Once operational, keep optimizing the solution's ability to find relevant service needs by refining the queries that pick up service based customer language.
6. If using people to categorize posts, adopt contact centre calibration techniques to ensure consistency.

Tips

- It's best to prioritize staff skills over tool selection – i.e. it's better to ensure your staff are properly trained and can implement basic Boolean search queries, than it is to spend money on a tool that creates these for you. It means you can spot data errors/omissions and fix them, and avoids the "black box" problem.*
- You should think about how you'll measure your monitoring success early on. This might be different from traditional channels and include percentage of queries responded to, change in positive vs negative sentiment, speed of query resolution, advocates created etc.*
- Build a search engine alert on "social media monitoring for Customer Service" to look out for the next better mousetrap. Stay alert for other classes of solution coming through e.g. corporate Big Data solutions or interaction analytics from the contact centre world.
- Build up your research library on social customer behaviour to augment the insights gained from your own monitoring. For instance, grab free

---

*Special thanks to Luke Brynley-Jones, co-founder of the UK's first social media consultancy and now CEO of OurSocialTimes for these best practice tips.

reports coming from listening platform vendors. These often score key organizations in a particular vertical market in how they use Facebook, Twitter or peer-to-peer support communities. Quite a few are listed in this book.

- Remember that automated surveillance is not a substitute for "being on the street". Regularly visit your own Twitter and Facebook sites and assess your responsiveness first hand.

4 The level of integration between social and traditional CS infrastructure supports effective operational management and our intended customer experience

Importance

Even if you opt for a "separatist" approach to evolving your Social Customer Service, you still need to consider its relationship with any "legacy" Customer Services infrastructure and assets. Joined-up service matters to customers. Their enduring priority is "make it simple, make it fast".

Thus cross-channel always trumps multi-channel for customer experience. So pay great attention when designing the customer journey if you are habitually encouraging customers to switch from public channels to private ones.

Consequences

If levels of integration remain at close to zero, most probably you will be doubling your workload, lack flexibility in resource planning and be unable to check against any 360° view of a customer's interaction history. In short, you are increasing the odds on depressing your customer experience ratings.

Correspondingly, a "one browser" strategy enables a "single version of the truth". This means any existing capabilities that are operationally required such as "unified queuing", access to enterprise systems (CRM/ Inventory) or to knowledge management assets are leveraged instead of being unnecessarily reinvented. Getting this right impacts both operational efficiency and effectiveness which directly translates into reduced customer effort and operational savings.

Issues

- Frequently transferring customers from Twitter and Facebook via direct messaging (DM) or private messaging (PM) is likely to be your weakest link if you then complete the service request on another infrastructure.
- You are missing vital operational expertise if you are still a Marketing/ PR led operation that does not involve your existing Customer Service management.
- Mainstream Customer Service infrastructure is designed to scale. When social volumes scale during a crisis how will you access this capability and any other pre-trained resources? Also how will you share the processes of listening, capturing, categorizing/reviewing, assigning and responding with other teams?
- Infrastructure for a peer-to-peer support community is largely independent of both contact centre and e-service. Think through whether this matters and in what customer scenarios you might need some level of integration (e.g. knowledge management). Some platforms offer integration options with Twitter and Facebook which are worth considering. These are explored in greater detail in Chapter 5.
- Beware the temptation to duplicate CRM and knowledge management functionality. This can apply as much to peer-to-peer community models as with Facebook and Twitter service channels. This needs careful thought when speccing any new Social Customer Service solution.
- Think about how you will want to use sources of customer data for service strategies. For instance what about the ability to track customer conversations across external media, including review sites, blogs, forums, Twitter, Facebook, YouTube videos, mainstream news sites and more, as well as the free form notes stored in internal sources such as CRM/contact centre notes, surveys and incoming emails, and relate those conversations to your internal data on sales figures, inventory numbers, Customer Service records and more. What integration implications does this kind of functionality have?

- Mainstream Customer Service vendors offering "socially enhanced" solutions offer the benefit of tight integration but may have an inferior feature set. Compare yours against native "best of breed" solutions to check if there is anything you absolutely must have.
- Separate infrastructures generate separate reporting. This means any global view of total Customer Service activity will have to be manually compiled.
- Your ability to understand how customers use both mainstream and social channels is made much harder when running two Customer Service infrastructures. This is especially significant if you discover social channel uptake is caused by failing to help customers via their original channel of choice. Aim to make these types of correlations as easy as operationally possible.

Quick wins version

One of the ways to reduce customer effort is to design integrated sign-posting for customers. This means promoting all channels on every channel. Include opening hours so customers can make informed choices. Photobox.com is an excellent example of how to do this. Also aim to make the journey from search engine to "right resource" as short as possible.

Follow up actions

1. Map your customer journeys and the service experience you want to provide. Understand where existing infrastructure and assets will be implicitly required. Consider your integration options in the light of those insights.
2. If you anticipate needing to transfer customers between service teams, get everyone in a room. Their task is to work out effective ways of briefing each other so that customer context is never dropped during transfer. Make this a big deal. Encourage operational slickness. Mystery shop the competency on a regular basis. Find and discuss publically

available examples of getting it wrong to maintain awareness of its importance within the teams.

3. If your strategy demands that service management teams are to remain separate, develop a programme that facilitates collaboration and mutual transfer of experience and best practice. Use such sessions to generate alignment (see question 6).

Tips

Draw a large map of the customer journey across all channels (cartoon style) and make sure it remains visible in every place you deliver service to make the point about unity of effort.

5 We know how to recruit, train and manage Social Customer Service teams

Importance

This topic can draw fierce debate and sometimes becomes a proxy fight between "old" and "new" ways. Some argue it is just a matter of finding people who are strong text based communicators. While others argue the whole nine yards around needing a "bean bag" culture and people that "get" social. It is therefore important to have developed your own carefully considered point of view based on understanding these different perspectives and underlying issues.

Consequences

Assuming you chose to see some degree of difference between the cultures of mainstream and Social Customer Service, it follows that the recruit-train-manage cycle is correspondingly different. Therefore success comes from recognizing and delivering against those differences. Equally, failure results from doing the same things as before while still expecting a fresh outcome.

However, it could be that you do not want to change any of the fundamentals. For instance, employee and customer feedback suggest your existing approach already works and there is no case for change. If this scenario fits then just "continue as normal".

Issues

- The long-standing advice around "not pouring new wine into old wine skins" can apply here. If you want to attract and retain the right talent, make sure you tune into current market perceptions around what being in the Social Customer Service business means to potential recruits. They might not come if the job offer is framed in traditional contact centre language. Thereafter they might not stay if placed in the culture and supervisory style of existing Customer Service. That said, some organizations have successfully positioned them as an elite team embedded within Customer Service as a role worth aspiring to in an advisor's career path. What's right for your organization?

- Make sure your induction programme is suitable. Think through what should remain from the existing version and what needs reinventing. For instance, consider the format. Contact centre induction is typically crammed into an intense, up front period, after which ongoing support is tightly rationed. Does that model work for the behaviours you want to encourage? Then think through the relevance of your content in the same way. Probably the "traditional" induction programme contains important guidance on corporate policy that needs to be carried over. Equally there are probably new topics such as corporate social media policies that have to be included For instance, have you a section on the legal ramifications of communicating on social networks? If you are encouraging a more authentic and personal style of interaction, what are the boundaries of acceptable and unacceptable social behaviour? How do you influence this? Once you start thinking it through, you discover there are plenty of issues that need tackling at the induction stage.

- Performance management of Social Customer Service teams also requires some serious thought. Non-Customer Service recruits probably won't welcome traditional performance expectations around tightly bounded time management and internally focused metrics. Also bear in mind that like customers, this type of person relates to social media broadly. It is more about customer engagement and less about whether it is labelled as a Marketing, Sales or Service communication.

    Some managers and supervisors will need to embrace a new mindset if they want to keep hold of this type of person.

- Sometimes Social Customer Service teams are expected to move heaven and earth in fixing things for the customer. This is probably already on top of compensating for shortfalls in poor mainstream service. Therefore if you are expecting your team to act as "sort anything out" ninjas, recognize this extra value in terms of pay, profile and internal status.

- Are you building any potential rivalry between mainstream and social service teams? If any real differences become known in terms of recognition and reward, make sure you provide careful explanation where needed.
- Some organizations issue social media guidelines for personal use. If these exist make sure your own guidelines for the Social Customer Service team are congruent.

Quick wins version

Mandate a cross-functional task force that ideally blends Customer Service and social media operational expertise to produce a "starter pack" version for use in the first six months of setting up a new team.

Follow up actions

1. Gather the best minds to debate the issue of any differences between existing and Social Customer Service teams. Link back to ownership debate in question 2.
2. Create appropriate job briefs and recruitment profiles. Remember roles in support communities need separate definition. Set remuneration to match role responsibilities. Define how roles fit in as part of a career path.
3. Establish and evangelize the Social Customer Service team's service mission, their internal positioning and mandate to help empower them.
4. Develop an appropriate induction and development strategy for all roles.
5. Review and upgrade the induction course material. Focus on specific communication skills for each of the platforms you intend operating on.
6. Review your performance and quality assurance framework to ensure it supports the development of desired behaviours. Tweak accordingly.

7. Frequently review the team's progress in the formative stages using customer and employee feedback. Use mystery shopping techniques to identify emerging best practice and areas of team/individual weakness. Network with other Social Customer Service leaders to access and swap learning.

Tips

- Talk to Social Customer Service team members (your own/others on site visits) and find out what they see as the similarities and differences in approach between social and traditional.
- Seek out recruiters and training partners who claim expertise in Social Customer Service and engage to find out what they know. Even use them if you are impressed!

6 We have aligned our Social Customer Service competencies with traditional ones

Importance

For some organizations that suffer deeply entrenched attitudes around Customer Service, running a separate team that discovers a "better" way can be an attractive transformation tactic. However, this does carry a certain risk if customers then notice a "back door" to getting their own service issues expedited. Any trends in Social Customer Service "successes" must be therefore examined for opportunities to improve mainstream service competencies. In other words, aim to "up your game" across all channels.

Consequences

The benefit of aligning competencies across channels is that you do not unconsciously create demand for an unscalable form of service. The downside of been caught out in this way is that the brand is seen to behave inconsistently – a major "sin" in any brand manager's book.

Issues

- Customers quickly learn how to exploit any gaps in the service experience to their advantage.

Quick wins version

Recruit a small team of employees to blind test your Social Customer Service team against mainstream versions. Debrief on the differences.

Follow up actions

- Have the various teams meet to discuss their approaches to Customer Service. Pick a common set of topics to structure the exploration. When differences exist consider if that matters and how any best practice is transferred. Keep the discussion as a frequent agenda item.

- Track improvement opportunities as part of the follow up from these sessions.

Tips

Use brand value statements as a common standard to unify the presentation styles of all the Customer Service channels in use.

7 We have identified our platform and the channel mix for Social Customer Service that works for the customer market(s) we operate in

Importance

There isn't a standard approach to providing Customer Service via social channels that you can just template. For instance a B2C property business might use a location based social network to show adjoining neighbourhoods for the properties they are renting. In New York where this example comes from, this is a known driver for sales conversion.

On the other hand, a consumer electronics business might choose a customer manned forum as the best way to provide up to date expertise. In their situation, choice is driven by their need to economically support a large portfolio of short life, complex products. So it all depends on the needs of your customers and your ability to find out what works for them.

Consequences

The positives of getting it right should be positive ROI on your platform and channel mix investment. Probable indicators include consistent customer use, regular achievement of whatever level of responsiveness is expected by your customers and high rates of first time resolution. All this should be reflected back in the customer feedback loop you run.

The negatives are underutilized presences on too many networks resulting in increased cost and/or diminished quality from overstretched resources and a lack of feel for the cultures of those individual social networks.

The issues

- The popularity of social networks rises and falls. Existing ones imitate each other's functionality and add new features to boost use. New networks continue to emerge. Meanwhile both customers and organizations find innovative ways of leveraging a social facility beyond its original purpose. Added together, this means change is constant. So a close eye is needed on:

- What's new
- If customer segments are likely to adopt them
- Any innovative uses that the organization can win kudos for (e.g. an airline seat reservations service based on matching passengers' social network connections).

Sometimes demand for providing service on a certain channel is created by your own organization's Sales and Marketing activities. As a rule of thumb, wherever you establish a Sales channel, the need for an associated service channel follows. So if you are active in selling on Facebook, customer demand for service will follow. Equally you might find that using Pinterest to visually promote part of your catalogue then starts to generate service related comments against certain pins.

- As we mentioned in Chapter 2, younger consumer groups expect to connect via a social network since it is second nature to them. These generational preferences for social interaction are likely to expand as younger siblings emerge as consumers in their own right. So review the demographics of your customer base.

Quick wins version

Research how your direct competitors organize their Social Customer Service. While their reasons might be unique or even not clearly thought through, they will provide a shortlist from which you can generate a "me too" service.

Follow up actions

- Map out your channel mix based on the output of question 3 and any examples from comparable organizations.

- Given the multiple benefits associated with running a support community for Customer Service, check out the customer case studies from the major solution providers for evidence of success in your market.
- Neither Twitter nor Facebook are ideal service environments. If you are destined to use them, look for ways to improve the customer experience. Some solution providers provide extra service functionality for Facebook. A dedicated Twitter account for service is currently a popular way to improve focus on service issues on that channel.
- Make sure you signpost all available service options on all channels as described in question 4 quick wins.
- Build a reporting capability that allows you to track trends in service traffic on all platforms you offer a service presence. Preferably with the ability to track cross-channel behaviour.

Tips

- Simple is best. Concentrate on getting excellent at a single social channel before opening another. If customers are on other networks, try linking from there to your "strong" service or even embed it.
- As the trend for adding visual content continues to grow, investigate the benefits of using video and/or desktop capture tools (e.g. Screenr) to provide education and self service assets. These can be curated in networks such as YouTube or Pinterest. This can be a very effective form of self service following a hand-off from a Twitter or Facebook interaction.
- In the way that organizations are learning to co-create with customers over products, why not incentivize the same willingness around service design? Try running a "best What, Where and Why service" campaign! Let them suggest what could work.

8 We have clearly mapped customer journeys for Social Customer Service based on their priorities

Importance

Organizations have powerful reasons for being motivated to get the customer journey working as expected. First is the fact that a proportion of interactions occur because existing Customer Service channels have failed. The customer is already inconvenienced and this can easily get worse if your responsiveness is weakened by:

- Missing or ignoring a service request
- Taking too long to reply
- Missing the next part in a conversation thread
- Failing to counter other customers/commentators seeking to influence a discussion.

Secondly, many customers are forced to move from their initial social channel of choice to another. One of the lessons from designing cross-channel customer journeys is the need to maintain simplicity and context. Otherwise customers end up repeating themselves and submitting to multiple identification sessions when being transferred. For obvious reasons, it is important to get this right in the transparent world of social interaction.

Consequences

Many organizations prematurely conclude that social interaction is too risky and therefore implement an immediate transfer policy. The impact of poorly thought through hand-offs can still be seen on certain Facebook sites as customers get bounced between social and mainstream Customer Service options.

On the other hand, proper thought and careful design around customer journeys should result in more service interactions staying "in channel" with a much smaller proportion that genuinely need confidentiality being handed off. The result would be less customer effort and the realization of one of social interaction's core benefits. Others can benefit from the interaction! As we know, part of the ROI in support communities is that answers are viewed multiple times. The final benefit is this. In a world when word of mouth carries more weight than any brand sponsored claim, customers are much more likely to leave a public thank you if the whole interaction has remained social.

Issues

- For many organizations, Social Customer Service has come to mean a Twitter and/or Facebook presence using a house style of immediately transferring the customer to a private channel. This is unlikely to meet customer priorities for "fast and easy" if extra complexity is added.
- Even though support communities have a reputation for converting difficult customers and developing "super users", it remains important to recognize how volatile customer sentiment can be if important support issues remain unsolved over a period. Therefore proactive communication is essential even when there is no real news. This can prevent a collapse of confidence in the channel as a place where "big" issues get sorted.

Quick wins version

Build a sample of most recent service users and ask them to critique their experience. Look for common points of failure and fix them.

Follow up actions

1. Find or hire expertise to map and then redesign all variations of the customer journey when the service request is initially made via a social channel.

2. Use the outputs of question 14 in this self-assessment to understand the detail of how customers expect social service to work.

Tips

- Model your customer journeys from their very start, e.g. beginning from a search engine rather than once they arrive at a social channel. This will remind you of signposting issues.
- Get your team familiar with every version of the customer journey so they live and breathe the customer's experience of the service, not an internal process view. Therefore name them, describe them, visualize them. Create language about them that allows people to relate and own them.

9 We are using socially sourced knowledge effectively and have access to relevant Customer Service knowledge

Importance

All forms of Customer Service are enriched by real-time access to customer data and relevant service knowledge. This has a direct bearing on how customers rate their service experiences. One of the "big" trends in using customer data is personalization. Although this encompasses all forms of customer engagement, it represents a great opportunity to differentiate service organizations when used effectively.

However, organizations must still remain sensitive to customer reaction in terms of how personal data is collected and used. Particularly when harvested from sources such as social networks. Boundaries are easily overstepped and differ according to regional regulation and national taste. Quite apart from how each individual might uniquely react.

The second topic in this competency is having the right answers on tap. Access to relevant Customer Service knowledge often becomes an issue when different support infrastructures are in use. In the worst case scenario, there could be knowledge silos built up in the contact centre, e-service, Facebook/Twitter and support community. This is clearly inefficient.

Consequences

Customer data

Being able to effectively personalize a service experience can improve both efficiency and effectiveness of a service operation. If you want to encourage customers to vocalize their gratitude then this is a strategy to adopt. However, inappropriate use of social profile data can alienate customers and may contravene local legislation.

Service knowledge

Effective cross-channel knowledge management improves service velocity and resolution rates. However, allowing each service channel to manage their own knowledge base without an overall strategy can result in customers receiving different answers within different channels.

Issues

- As consumers become increasingly used to the personalization of their digital world, the odds increase that they expect similar treatment in their service experiences.
- Consumer attitudes around what brands know about them are polarized. Research shows they do not like being "listened" to online despite the fact they expect relevant interventions when they have an issue. See Chapter 2 for details. Organizations need to show ongoing EQ (emotional intelligence) as the privacy debate continues to unfold.
- Celebrity status customers bring with them huge followings. The quality of their service experience often has immediate consequences in terms of mass commentary by their followers. Examples show this is true for even the most mundane domestic issue! Being able to spot them and prioritize their needs makes sense from a brand management perspective.
- Some customers love to complain. Social forums act as oxygen for them. Examples show extreme serial complainers can even sustain 100+ posts a day. Checking their activity on other sites can be a useful way of profiling their behaviour and deciding if they warrant remaining your customers.
- A common source of social profile data comes in the form of influence scores which are often baked into Social Customer Service workflow solutions as a way of prioritizing service requests. This is another topic that causes heated debate. Are all customers equal? Or are some more so than others? Experts meanwhile question the validity of these metrics. Research the topic and decide for yourself.

- Service knowledge sourced from customer manned forums tends to be generated outside the editorial-legal vetting loop that many organizations prefer to use to generate service knowledge. How will these be aligned? At what point can this source of knowledge be shared across other channels?

Quick wins version

Run a weekly session with the Social Customer Service team to identify latest knowledge gaps. Also get them to report back on previous topics now researched and available.

Follow up actions

1. Check what social profile data is being used already by Marketing and whether it is appropriate for Customer Service.
2. Check on whether there is relevant legislation on personal data within the territories where you operate (especially if you provide a centralized pan European support service).
3. If there is a personalization strategy as part of your organization's digital marketing strategy, consider translating that into a service context (align with previous action).
4. Co-ordinate a common approach around service knowledge management with other Customer Service teams.
5. Do a gap analysis of what service knowledge is needed. Check if answers exist in other service silos.
6. Track most commonly asked questions being raised on your social channels in order to find examples that can be transformed into FAQs/instructional videos/infographic style datasheets. Make sure these are shared with any other Customer Service teams.

    Within your support forums, set up metrics to track answer "quality", stickiness, bounce rates of content and community links. Link back to call deflection targets.

7. If video becomes a major form of self service delivery, consider developing in-house capability within the service team. It's cheaper and faster.

Tips

Instead of trying to centralize all service knowledge think about providing a common search capability across all sources. This is called federated search.

10 We are able to build and access social interaction history as needed

Importance

Providing Customer Service teams with desktop/tablet access to a customer's interaction history provides context and injects relevance to any current exchange. It also informs routing decisions whether automated or through human moderation.

Consequences

Providing access to all sources of interaction history enables a personalized service (when relevant) and a common corporate "memory" across every channel. The downside of not being able to access any form of interaction history is the danger of customers repeatedly describing their situation (more so when being handed off to a new channel).

Issues

- If separate and non-integrated infrastructures are being used between social and mainstream Customer Service teams, interaction histories are likely to be siloed. Therefore the organization remains blind to a customer's total cross-channel behaviour. Given the fact that customers resort to social channels after an unsuccessful encounter via another channel, it puts the advisor on the front foot knowing what has already happened.
- Another reason for being able to aggregate interaction history is economic. Do you know who drives your service traffic? For instance a UK telco discovered 20% of service volumes came from just 1.5% of their customer base.
- High value customers who actively prefer using a social channel to do business can find themselves repeating their credentials, e.g. each time

providing a frequent flyer ID and email. This undermines the brand promise of VIPs being valued.

- Assuming you intend to collect interaction histories in the main CRM system, make sure the customer template is adapted to include social profile data (e.g. Twitter handle) and that interaction history can be referenced back to its social channel.

Quick wins version

Use your social media monitoring system to identify the top 5% of customers using your social channels. Provide a cheat sheet of their names so that advisors are more likely to recognize them. Refresh every three months.

Follow up actions

1. Check if your intended Social Customer Service solution has some form of database capability to store and therefore recall interaction history. By the way, the ability to see interaction history in a support community format is easy. Simply click through to a customer's profile for an overview of their posts.
2. Find out the cost and viability of integrating social interaction histories with the main CRM system.

Tips

Run quarterly sessions to examine a cross-section of customer interaction histories. What do they tell you about your service effectiveness, the original need for service, the type of customers that most often use a social channel? Feed this back into your service tactics.

11 We are ready for unexpected volumes of "social" traffic: Resourcing, escalation, house style

Importance

People who are in the know will tell you that dealing with a social media crisis is not a matter of if but when. Any organization can find themselves tripped up either through their own design or others'. On some days, that might not be noticed. On another day the conditions are such that the issue goes viral. Welcome to the world of "faster than real-time" crisis management. Given the inevitability of this happening and the fact it cannot be anticipated, extensive planning and rehearsal are needed.

Consequences

If you are prepared, you will be able to scale to meet demand, match and even influence the mood of those discussing your situation and possibly come out the other end with greater kudos and brand reputation than before the storm.

If you are ill prepared, you are likely to be constantly on the back foot as the organization's chain of command attempts to respond. You are likely to get caught out if saying anything other than the truth and it will inflame and perpetuate the situation. If you appear unable to respond, are indifferent, too corporate, too slow or too flippant, this will be used against you. After the event passes, you are likely to suffer brand damage at the very least. Many suffer direct commercial loss as well.

Issues

- The speed at which situations unfold means there is little time for traditional command and control style response. In reality the front line has to be ready to do the heavy lifting plus whatever expertise is networked into operational decision making. This implies you have developed a trusted, capable and empowered team of communicators from the moment you wrote their recruitment brief.

- The use of social media monitoring is essential to track trending topics and volume of activity. Make sure this can be activated without issue in these circumstances and made available to the tactical response team.

- Ensure "real-time" means just that with your social monitoring vendor. Especially Twitter.

- A crisis can occur any time of day, any day of the week. While some markets have always needed to have a 365x24 response capability, this will be a new requirement for others. If this is true for you, how will this be resourced?

- There are different types of crises. This can affect how Customer Services becomes involved. The most relevant category is a "big" service issue. Examples could be a sustained network outage affecting mobile phones or online banking, a severe weather event or natural disaster that impacts customer safety or travel plans, a product issue that threatens the safety or health of consumers. In these cases Customer Services would normally play the lead role. In other examples such as a hacked database of confidential customer data or a scandal involving the whole brand, Customer Services may play a support role behind a PR lead. The way in which crisis plans are developed needs to recognize these different scenarios.

- It's a fact that employees move on and crisis tactics evolve as more examples provide new lessons. Therefore make sure the plan is regularly revisited, trained resources remain available and the key behaviours in the plan are actively rehearsed in as authentic a way as possible to maintain "crisis" fitness.

Quick wins version

Plan a very simple version based on a fabricated deadline that you need to be ready within the next five days. Given that, what would you focus on?

Follow up actions

1. Find out if any crisis plans already exist.
2. Research lessons learned from previous crises played out on social networks.
3. Brainstorm Customer Service scenarios and response guidelines.
4. Define roles, accountabilities and escalation triggers.
5. Develop a resourcing strategy. This could involve an ongoing internal recruitment drive for "part time" volunteers. If so think through how they are provisioned with the right systems.
6. Develop a training plan.
7. Plan how social media monitoring is made available to the team. Confirm its suitability, i.e. that it is truly real-time and especially that the Twitter feed is instant. If not make provision for a specialist crisis monitoring platform.
8. Rehearse regularly.
9. Review recent examples with the team for lessons learned. Update plan accordingly.

Tips

Keep the plan simple. Concentrate more on rehearsing and learning from those experiences.

12 We have the right balance of metrics that reflect both the customers' priorities and those of operational management

Importance

Customer service metrics matter because they drive behaviour and ROI. Traditional Customer Service metrics have been evolving towards a more customer centred view of service quality. Add to this the realization within the service industry that focusing on effectiveness is just as important as efficiency. Social Customer Service needs to balance this mainstream agenda with a new generation of social media metrics. Of course the context for selecting the "right" metrics is the strategic service goals you have set. See question 1.

Consequences

The impact of measuring the wrong things is already a well discussed topic in the contact centre industry. Often this has been driven by what can be measured as opposed to what is valuable to measure. Consumer perception of service and quality standards has suffered as a result. Social Customer Service teams need to learn from these lessons.

The upside of getting a balanced set of metrics in place is that you are reacting to the right issues and are able to learn and improve. Done consistently, this will produce a win-win for customers, front line teams and the organization. This is the route to discovering your ROI for Social Customer Service.

Issues

- Leaders of Social Customer Service teams need to be aware of how their views might impact this debate. Those coming from a Marketing/PR background should still seek to learn from their contact centre colleagues about operational metrics even if they hold strong views about the service experience they perceive contact centres deliver. Equally, those from a contact centre background should avoid any wholesale implementation of traditional metrics and expand their horizons around "newer" metrics and associated social business strategies.

- Integrated reporting is still some generations away. Possible source include:
  - External sources such as Bitly style link tracking or Facebook Insights
  - Social media monitoring platforms
  - Workflow solution
  - CRM system
  - Contact centre platform
  - Community support platform.
- If you are lucky some of these might be rolled up into a pre-integrated solution. Or you might work for an organization that is good at data management and will provide you with a real-time dashboard that mashes up these diverse data sources. Even then "complex" metrics such as cross-channel resolution rates are likely to be manual exercises. So plan to resource this effort accordingly and aim to keep your metrics to an effective minimum.
- Support community managers have their own set of measurement challenges. Typical ones include calculating the real impact on call deflection, assessing the number of times a customer answer has solved other customers' needs and measuring the effectiveness of published "knowledge".
- Service metrics are only valuable in the context of strategic business goals. Don't let one exist without the other.

Quick wins version

Simply focus on these three metrics:

- Responsiveness (did we respond)
- Timeliness (how long we took to respond)

- Impact/Gratitude Index* (percentage of unsolicited thanks from customers).

Follow up actions

1. List your strategic goals for Customer Service and any specifically for Social Customer Service.
2. Gather a list of metrics from existing Customer Service activity. Download and study the list of metrics provided in the TELUS whitepaper called *Measuring Social Customer Service in the Contact Center | Metrics & ROI for Social Care* released March 2012. Select those that relate to your strategic goals. Fill in any gaps. Review the balance between internal and external focus.
3. Double check using this simple three-step guide:
   (a) Given your strategic goals, what core questions do you need to be asking to ensure success?
   (b) What information do you need to answer those questions?
   (c) What metrics are therefore needed?
4. Define your data gathering and reporting needs. Find the right internal experts to advise how this can be operationalized.

Tips

Build a personal network of Social Customer Service managers from equivalent organizations. Learn what they have done around metrics.

---

*Thanks to Jerome Pineau for inspiring this quick win.

13 Our SLAs for serving customers via social channels outperform competition

Importance

The way this competency is expressed assumes you are motivated to be the best. Maybe even build your service capability to become a reason why customers choose your organization. Given that here is the question. Is your service remarkable?*

SLAs (service level agreements) are where the rubber hits the road as far as customers are concerned. How fast, how easy, how well informed, how well understood. These things matter to customers. However, please make sure you focus on the right ones. What organizations think are customer priorities often do not match reality.

Also remember that competition comes in many forms. Direct competitors are certainly one benchmark. However, customers' points of reference are as broad as their experience. In a global, socially networked economy, expectations for what great service means can be changed overnight. Being distinctively good these days is a marathon at a brisk trot.

Consequences

The first phase of Social Customer Service was distinguished by lousy SLA performance levels via Twitter and Facebook. Support communities are less of an eyesore since they don't survive for long unless they function effectively. They either deliver or die off.

So, unless the whole argument around the impact of poor service on customer behaviour is massively overhyped and the real truth is that

---

*Thanks to Seth Godin for this question.

customers don't really care, it follows that non-performing Social Customer Service teams will find themselves punished.

Conversely, the impact of getting it right all depends on what your insight into customer behaviour tells you. How important is good service to their purchasing behaviour, their WOM (word of mouth) behaviour? This will tell you where the bar needs setting.

Issues

- It takes time and investment to reach a remarkable level of service. While that might be a personal motivator, make sure you win organizational backing for that journey
- SLAs are market specific. For instance a bank can offer a 9–5/5 day week service and still satisfy expectation. Equally an airline has to provide rapid response on a 24x7x365 basis since time is of the essence in that industry. That said, the digital world we live in is trending towards real-time. So here is a rule of thumb. If a direct competitor opens longer, responds faster, you probably need a great reason not to follow suit.

Quick wins version

Become familiar with competitor performance. Identify where their customers react most strongly when they underperform. Focus on becoming better in those situations. Then promote that superior capability.

Follow up actions

1. Use your social media monitoring reports to understand the patterns in customer communication, e.g. over a 24-hour period, weekly, monthly and year-on-year cycles. Consider implications for SLAs and resourcing.

2. Develop a post interaction feedback programme, part of which probes what really matters to customers as a service experience. Make this a channel specific exercise to compare any differences of expectation. For instance, speed of response might be characteristic of Twitter channel users while quality of knowledge might be the prime driver for support community users. Model your SLAs on those insights.
3. Make sure you have the right metrics in place to track SLAs (see previous competency question 12).
4. Consider who else benefits from SLA reporting. Enable browser based access for them.

Tips

Avoid the temptation to measure SLA progress on the basis of average performance. It is by addressing the outliers that you will end up with superior performance.

14 We have a sufficiently detailed understanding from customer feedback to know what does and does not work about our social channels

Importance

In the days when "nobody could hear you scream in the IVR", it took longer for the word to get out that your service sucks. Not so these days. Service is now a spectator sport, witnessed by the many. Ignorance is no longer a plausible excuse. So closing the loop to really listen, learn and improve is what any sane organization ought to be getting on with.

Consequences

At present there is little evidence that organizations are attempting any form of quality assurance or are listening to customers about the quality of their Social Customer Service. The road to enlightenment on this topic is being able to distinguish that active listening and automated monitoring are in fact quite different activities and therefore have different outcomes.

That said, mainstream Customer Service has recently woken up to the improvement opportunity that post interaction surveys and interaction analytics provide. As is so often said, *"if you can't measure it, you can't improve it"*. In other words, you run the risk of being "unconsciously incompetent".

The upsides of tying together customer feedback with an improvement workflow (question 15) are that regular visitors no longer witness the same issues over and over. Secondly, service improvement becomes a promotional opportunity. Imagine that.

Issues

- One of the enduring issues for Customer Service leaders is to check you have an accurate view of the customer experience. Numerous studies have shown just how different internal perceptions can become from those of actual customers. Internal agendas exert a powerful influence, particularly when bonuses and other incentives are tied into customer scores. It can be equally beguiling when organizations enter and win industry recognition for "great service". There are many ways organizations end up believing their own PR. However, the transparency of Social Customer Service raises the stakes. Take heed.

- Being able to evaluate the customer experience becomes more complex when the initial enquiry is handed off to another channel or team such as mainstream Customer Services.

Quick wins version

Assuming the right cultural context, what about incentivizing advisors and team leaders to immediately message a percentage of customers as soon as their case is concluded? Ask them what mattered most to them in making this form of Customer Service a successful experience.

Follow up actions

1. Research whether there is any existing initiative (e.g. Voice of The Customer) to provide expertise and/or toolsets.
2. Consider your feedback options. Post interaction surveying, interaction analytics, social media monitoring, Gratitude Index (see Tips).
3. Think beyond feedback and include the whole improvement cycle. Work out how the feedback is to be practically used in operational management.

Tips

- Talk less. Listen more.
- Set up a Gratitude Index. This tracks unprompted praise by customers. Maybe the purest form of feedback. This is how to set one up:

- "Gratitude" is defined as containing one or more of these keywords in a tweet or post. "Thanks", "thx", "thank you", "tuvm", "appreciate". Invite other organizations you want to include in the Index. Then on a like-for-like basis use the same monitoring platform to listen out for those phrases. The Gratitude Index is the percentage of mentions out of all service interactions for each participating organization. Of course you can run the Index just for yourself.
- As soon as you start to make regular improvements resulting from the feedback, consider the value of actively promoting these on the relevant channel. The underlying message is that we listen, we learn and your feedback is worth offering.

15 We are able to learn from social interactions and track improvements

Importance

The visibility of social interaction between customers and organization provides a ready-made source of improvement opportunities. Traditionally Customer Service has had a tough time proving the root cause of service failure and getting things fixed. This is now changing as interaction analytics and "Big Data" solutions arrive. Social Customer Service data adds further momentum to this trend.

We are now entering the age in which Customer Service provides a mirror for the rest of the organization to see itself. This elevates Customer Service into a key strategic role in customer orientated organizations. Those in Social Customer Service can only benefit.

Consequences

The upsides are numerous. Operational costs are reduced as service failure volumes decline. Customer satisfaction improves as customer effort is minimized. Beyond improvement lies innovation. Mature deployments of support communities are well known for capturing, evaluating and benefiting from customer ideas.

Conversely, failure to learn can affect brand reputation over time. The chances of this becoming corrosive to customer sentiment increases the more that people witness a brand's failure to act.

Issues

- The Social Customer Service team might not have the bandwidth to do much more than operationally respond to customer issues. If that's the case then certain issues that could be fixed are likely to be repeated.

- It is known from mainstream Customer Service that the majority of opportunities for service improvement exist outside their direct control. In other words they are caused by other teams. These are the ones who need convincing that change is needed. Indicative keyword reports or senior reaction to a "live" situation might be sufficient to trigger a change in process or policy. This cannot be relied on. Unfortunately social analytics is not typically geared to archiving historic data for mining the frequency and size of an issue and therefore quantifying the value of solving it. Deployment of interaction analytics in contact centres has shown this is a vital part of business case development when significant change is at stake.
- Even when it is easier to evidence the need for improvement, e.g. the volume of posts accumulating on a single issue in a support community, it is often the personal network of relationships that the community leadership team have built that then facilitates these changes happening as opposed to more formal channels.
- When change is implemented, there is no guarantee that everything is then fixed. The old issue might resurface. There may be unintended consequences generated by the new solution. Having the resources and ability to track improvements is necessary for effective change management.

Quick wins version

Run a monthly session with contact centre, e-service and Social Customer Service teams to spot common opportunities and issues. Between sessions, use simple team based voting to track if improvements are being sustained.

Follow up actions

1. Build an approach to gathering insights from customer interactions that works for your resource and budget levels. Ask your social media monitoring vendor how they can help. Keep a close watch on any

complementary analytics capability being introduced elsewhere in your organization.

2. Align team goals, metrics and rewards to make this activity part of everyday work.

3. Develop a tracking system that allows you to effectively monitor improvements.

4. Promote this mission across the business. Build a network of support. Maintain awareness of its value through internal marketing. Plug into any other related initiatives such as Voice of the Customer (VoC).

Tips

- Successful social media leaders have made it their business to proactively network at equivalent levels. In times of need, when fixes are required, often at short notice, this investment pays off.
- Incentivize the Social Customer Service teams to keep personal journals on what they notice as common themes in their interactions. Use these as inputs to more formal analysis.

Summary

As promised, Chapter 4 is a thorough examination of what it takes to effectively manage customer experience and corporate reputation over social channels. If you have managed to complete the assessment form you will have three columns filled in.

The timeframe options allowed you to think in both short and medium-term horizons. Start with the short-term view. Recheck all the suggested quick wins and no doubt all the other ideas you jotted down. Now paint your 12-month roadmap. After that, think about the key themes you are tackling and the priority competencies you need to bring about. Turn them into your initial set of strategic aims. We suggest no more than six.

Take a break and when you return go back to the quick wins and think about the broader agenda that sits behind them. Without necessarily putting them against a timeline, articulate them as part of your strategy so they remain top of mind. Also isolate any competencies that received a low score on current standing, yet scored higher in terms of organizational importance. Some of those are probably priorities.

All that should give you a pretty good idea of what you need to be getting on with. It is then all about implementation. All the active practitioners we have come across and talked with work in a highly iterative and responsive way. For them strategy is dynamic and discovered by doing.

That said they are all veterans with at least half a dozen years and a few brands under their belts. Unless you sit in that company, there is no shame in a bit of planning!

Chapter 5

Using Peer-to-Peer Support in Your Service Strategy

"What happens when we treat customers as part of the company?"

This question is still one of our all-time favourites. It's catalytic and to the point. In fact, you can transform an entire organization just by following through on its logic. It was posed by Lyle Fong, Chief Strategist and Co-Founder of Lithium, one of the major platform providers of peer-to-peer support.

This chapter explores how these communities work, their benefits, how they fit with your other social channels and where the market for peer-to-peer support is heading.

Of course, organizations have been using online communities for over twenty years. In that time, some have matured into major hubs for customer engagement, offering rich insight to a wide range of functional teams. Smart organizations use them as the centrepiece of their VoC (Voice of the Customer) efforts.

Communities allow customers and organizations to get closer. Whatever your position on customer loyalty, communities have proved one of the best ways of nurturing abiding relationships. They exist and endure through the shared interest of their membership. It is they who operationally run the community, source its knowledge, generate its discussions and share its governance with the organization who typically acts as sponsor.

> "We found that the more we connected people to each other and connected them to us, the stronger the engagement online, the stronger the brand loyalty became."
>
> Bian Salins – Head of Social in the TV & Media industry. Previously Head of Social for a Telcomms company

Peer-to-peer support emerged out of this overall community based market. Sometimes it happened as a natural part of the dialogue within existing communities. In these cases support became a recognized function within a much broader community mission. However, new platforms also came to market specifically tailored for Customer Service duties. In organizations without any prior form of community, this proved to be a great step forward.

Branded peer-to-peer support is often an evolutionary response to what an organization's customers are already doing: helping each other out. This could be in a discussion thread on a review site, a blog or any of the specialist forums.

Many organizations get this is happening the first time they plug in their social monitoring and start listening. Often those that now offer peer-to-peer support initially discovered their customers were indeed seeking help elsewhere – more often than not, because their own efforts had fallen short.

There can be many reasons for this:

■ Some organizations overvalue Sales at the expense of Service and so simply do not put in enough effort to organize an effective response. Customers know this and go elsewhere for help.

- Some organizations find they are always behind the knowledge curve. Thus certain expert customers will always be better informed than an in-house resource.
- Some organizations cannot afford to match the level of community responsiveness that can be ticking 24x7.

The decision to consolidate this dispersed customer effort into a branded community has made sense to a lot of organizations. In a world that prizes customer engagement and speaks of crowdsourcing and co-creation, it's a practical way forward.

The typical evolutionary path is to quietly open a community style support service and let the customers discover its value. In the early days the organization provides most of the answers to the first generation of visitors, many of whom will not return until they have another question.

Some though are drawn in and involve themselves answering other customers' questions and having fun sharing their expertise. The most prolific can be motivated to devote significant time to becoming a recognized and respected contributor of that community.

These "super users" become the life blood of the community and enable the organization to take an indirect support role in order to concentrate on other aspects of support management. This can include anything from driving cross-functional improvement issues to knowledge curation as the volume of answers grows and the complexity of making it readily available becomes more challenging.

Community dynamics – why it works

One of the ways a "social archaeologist" would be able to date a certain period in the last sixty years is by the look and feel of its software.

Twenty years ago, text based forums were a first generation approach to "ask a question" and "find an answer". They were hard to search and navigate. Search engines were mainly blind to their content. Newcomers typically leafed through out of date (non-dynamic) FAQs called "stickies". They wasted time hunting up and down lists of sub-forums and threads. Some, based on temperament, just dived straight in with a "newbie" question. This often received a ticking off for not looking in the right place.

Fast forward to today's versions and much has been learned in terms of how to present information, (embedded multi-media, word clouds), make it more discoverable (tags, SEO and federated search) and facilitate users to easily join in (social logins and social sharing). All this is wrapped up in the now familiar UI expected of a modern social network able to scale to any screen size.

From this perspective, things look quite different. We have moved on. As in the equivalent of, "today's smartphone has the same horsepower as a laptop from the previous decade". Underneath the surface though, community behaviour has not changed to the same degree. In fact it has remained remarkably consistent.

As the social archaeologist well knows, humans are a predictable lot in terms of how we like to fit in. Thus there are three stable forms of participation in any online community. The 90/9/1 is a well known rule of thumb in community dynamics.

- 90% of all users are "lurkers". They read, search, navigate and observe, but don't contribute.
- 9% of all users contribute occasionally.
- 1% of all users participate a lot and account for most of the content in the community.

This means a small fraction of hyper contributors produce a substantial amount of the community content which then sustains the majority. This is the basis on which you build and operate peer-to-peer support.

"For community to work you need people that find success in the appreciation that comes from being helpful. All I did was to allow them to be more helpful. I reached into the wider business to get information that was only privy to the internal organisation, which the business felt comfortable giving to these trusted customers. That itself piqued their interest. The next step was these customers knowing the community management team. Putting a face to the names, spending time with them, that consolidated engagement further. Once you have a core group on board it encourages the rest of the community to want to participate."

Bian Salins – Head of Social in the TV & Media industry.
Previously Head of Social for a Telcoms company

This is how the so-called "super users" arise. When this behaviour is deployed in a service context, an entirely new kind of issue resolution takes place. Take giffgaff, the SIM only UK mobile brand. Vincent Boon, their community manager, summed up the dynamic like this:

"Our super users are spending upwards of 170 hours a month helping the community to answer questions and assisting people migrating onto our service. Some giffgaffers even spent over nine hours a day helping people."

Source: **Lithium giffgaff Case Study Using Community to Build an Entirely New Kind of Company 2011**

Of course it takes skill and commitment to develop this level of involvement. Community managers will tell you there is no such thing as treading water. You are either expanding or contracting in perceived value. There is much to be done making a community tick.

That said, advocates of the peer-to-peer support model claim the approach is faster, cheaper and often more effective in terms of first time resolution and quality of generated knowledge relative to traditional

Customer Service strategies. Naturally customer satisfaction, however, measured, also trends higher than average.

However, it is important to be clear when peer-to-peer works best. For instance classic Customer Service issues such as stock availability or delivery issues should still be answered by an organization's employees. They have the relevant data.

The value of customer involvement comes into its own around topics they really understand. How a product is actually used. This is always something that designers, manufacturers and retailers of products have comparatively little insight into once customers have purchased. How their products or services are actually used or consumed in daily life disappears from view.

This is where customers become the experts. They use it, abuse it, re-invent it, take it apart, find the things that don't work. Notice the things that should be there. In other words their community value extends from simple fixes to what is sometimes called "ideation" – creative input for your product roadmap.

In fact, the more complex your product, the more valuable this type of input becomes.

For instance, brands that offer complex software have long understood it is their customers who drive the value. They discover how the software works in practice, what it enables, how to get around the shortcuts of the current release, what best practice looks like.

Vendors such as SAP, Microsoft, and Autodesk have learned how to get out of the way and let their customers network, share expertise and learn from each other. As testament to their value, some of these communities have membership in the hundreds of thousands, occasionally in the millions.

They work because it is a deep human instinct to use communities and be part of them. In fact, this current phase of internet evolution is just that. The so-called "social web" is all about experimenting with community dynamics such as accelerating innovation, socializing issues, spreading ideas, extending influence.

One of the interesting trends coming out of all this is the gradual fusion of these longer standing, branded communities with the much larger, more fluid communities that form in and around the major social networks. We have of course been here before. AOL's walled garden lost its appeal as the first generation of internet services diverted its members' attention and everyone went "online".

Ironically the appeal of the walled garden has returned. Only this time with a zen koan style cunning that to "trap a bull, you need to place him in such a large field, he does not notice his incarceration". All the major social networks have their own walled garden policy to encourage members to "sit happily in the centre of the field". However, as we well know, their services come at a price. Our information is rarely entirely private. At best it is shared with the platform owner. It can even be owned by them.

This does have implications for organizations who want to control who else benefits from their crowdsourcing efforts. It is one of the reasons why these branded communities manage to survive even when "everyone is on Facebook". In their annual review of traditional communities, ComBlu, a social business and influencer marketing firm, makes the following point:

"Overall, the biggest miss that we observed this year is the lack of comprehensive community and social assimilation. Many brands continue to define Facebook as their community and point to the number of fans or likes as an indicator of community success. Yet countless studies have concluded that 'likes' are not equivalent to 'relationships with customers.' In reality, a social-only strategy is an incomplete line of attack, as is a 'branded community-only' approach. The two are symbiotic and contribute to overall engagement. It is important for brands to understand what to do where and optimize the natural leverage between the owned and social infrastructure."

Source: **ComBlu, The State Of Online Branded Communities 2012**

The stand-off is not confined to traditionalists in community management. Indeed they are a few voices out there who strongly criticize the use of social networks for any form of Customer Service because of who ultimately controls the platform. Whether this will prove "wise counsel" in an age of Software as a Service (SaaS) and all manner of cloud services remains to be seen.

No doubt, the future balance between a location based, membership driven model versus a virtualized, social ID sign-on model will depend on what drives each community. Those whose discussions and insights are reserved for their own membership will want to stay closer to the traditional model. Those who want to amplify their activity such as the peer-to-peer support model will happily embrace the new mindset. In this context it boosts your service mission when users "like" a post or share it with friends on other social networks.

Another well-known platform vendor, Get Satisfaction, puts it this way:

"It used to be enough to have your community on the Internet. Now, however, your community needs to be everywhere your customers are."

And the best way to do that is "Go Social".

How peer-to-peer support fits with other channels and support infrastructure

Although peer-to-peer support communities can grow into a rich ecosystem of live assistance, self service, search and the like, they start out in life and can remain divorced from other channels, Customer Service assets and mainstream organizational workflow. As we know from the self-assessment process in Chapter 4, our end game has to be some form of cross-channel capability. So what are the options for integrating peer-to-peer support?

Well assuming budget, time and capability are no constraints, deeper integration is almost certainly possible on a bespoke basis. However, this brings its own problems such as repeated integration costs and downtime with each new release of the core platform. So that route is not ideal.

Happily, the peer-to-peer vendor community has been busy and now provides a wide range of pre-integrated options. This has updated the value and relevance of their core platforms and made them fit for the kind of socially orientated, distributed functionality now common in modern software design.

The following functionality is now typical of all the leading vendors and should be considered as standard criteria if you are in the process of evaluating a new platform or upgrading.

Peer-to-peer support is no longer just a destination which requires signposting. As previously mentioned, customers no longer need to find your community. It can come to where they are. This is enabled via widget architecture wherever it makes sense. This means you can easily embed relevant customer conversations anywhere on your website or Facebook property. This increases the exposure of your community assets to a whole new audience who might never consider using a community.

Let's first explore an e-commerce integration. Imagine each listed product on the site now has its own relevant support questions next to it. This provides potential customers with more context relevant information for their decision making. The same tactic could also be mirrored at check-out to reduce cart abandonment rates. This in itself would probably pay for the functionality many times over!

Let's move on to consider a full omni-channel example. Mobile users could access relevant peer-to-peer resources when in a retail store via a barcode/QR code attached to the products. Retailers would add these to augment peer product reviews as part of their overall efforts to counteract show-rooming.

These are just a few examples of how you can now project the community to wherever it benefits your customers. Let's move on to other examples of how to build out your Social Customer Service ecosystem with peer-to-peer support at its centre.

Peer-to-peer platforms also offer easy integration with leading CRM providers. This means you can leverage what you already know about a customer and extend that insight by merging their community activity back into the CRM database.

Here is an example of how that could be used in designing service strategies. Imagine using CRM data to authenticate customers as they log in. This would then enable you to link a subscription based support service with "free" peer-to-peer services as part of your delivery strategy.

Autodesk describes this approach in their 2012 Lithy award submission. Interestingly the NPS scores for their peer-to-peer support rivalled all but the top level of their paid subscription service. Yet according to their own calculations, the cost of delivering a peer-to-peer support service relative to a technical 1:1 interaction was 1,000 cheaper!

CRM vendors such as Salesforce offer even richer capability than just access to CRM data. For instance, through their extended ecosystem, you can tap into case management functionality and rules based escalation. This would allow you to design different customer journeys. For example:

- By type of customer
- Any new trending topic that requires urgent attention
- Customer questions that have remained unanswered that now breach a community SLA (service level agreement) and require escalation.

Of course since the escalated case is now visible via a cloud enabled CRM desktop, this can be made available via custom workflows to wherever the right expertise sits within your organization. Answers can then be posted back to the community from that desktop. This can be a powerful way to collaborate around those "big" issues that land in the community every so often and demand co-ordinated internal response beyond the know-how of even super users.

And when case resolution becomes complex by either taking more time or involving a number of separate interactions, customers can also benefit from being routed to the same advisor and in between times be kept updated on progress. In other words, advanced workflow and notifications can now be readily layered on top of peer-to-peer support to provide social strategists with yet more design options.

One of the great assets that a support community generates is its knowledge. So it is well worth considering how to make best use of it. For a start it is typically generated more rapidly and is more valued by users than the internally scripted and vetted knowledge which traditional e-service and contact centre service teams have had to rely on.

This begs the question of how it can become more widely used outside the community environment. Previously we mentioned the power of widgets to make community assets available wherever needed. What else is possible?

Let's start where most customers will start, using a search engine. If they immediately find community answers being listed from their initial search, you are effectively sharing those answers in the widest, most comprehensive way.

This can be achieved through a combination of SEO friendly platforms that encourage search engines to index their content and value added community administration in terms of extra tagging and keyword indexing to make content even more discoverable. Get this right and customers can be just two clicks away from finding what they are looking for arriving at exactly the right place in the community.

Another tactic is to use a combination of federated search and links. Together they help make social content and real-time FAQs from your support community visible within online help sections and on advisor desktops. This can be further leveraged by encouraging advisors to embed links within their responses when dealing with Twitter and Facebook sourced enquiries. Thus customers find answers from their peers and are introduced to the community.

While we are on the topic of leveraging social knowledge there is another source to consider. What about those support interactions taking place on the likes of Twitter and Facebook? While social media is gaining SEO prominence, the "half-life" of social media content remains very brief unlike the content you can control in your branded support community. Its value can easily disappear from view especially on Twitter.

Instead of being managed according to someone else's data policies, that knowledge asset needs to be transformed into persistent and discoverable content that your organization owns. Some vendors provide the option of bringing these one-off conversations into your community so that helpful but fleeting content is preserved as a long-lasting community resource.

By the way, some experts argue that Google+ communities pose a similar challenge. It is a one size fits all solution which is entirely self-contained. While it might continue to add functionality, it is not designed to readily integrate with a wider support ecosystem. That includes any community-generated knowledge. Moreover you are subject to Google's terms and conditions and in theory could have your service channel cancelled without notice. They might even cancel the platform. They do have a history of terminating new ventures. So think carefully if you are tempted to use it as your central community platform.

So exactly how does peer-to-peer support fit in with Facebook and Twitter activities? Let's start with Facebook. A separate help page is the current way in which Facebook users are most commonly linked with community resources. Questions either receive relevant community answers or are routed for live response by community members. The US telco Sprint does this.

In a similar way tweets can be pushed to the community for unrestricted discussion and resolution. In either case, outstanding tweets and Facebook posts can be escalated as previously mentioned to an advisor or community moderator if not picked up by a community user.

It is also easy for the social network user to register as a community member by simply using their relevant social ID. This then allows them to share community posts with their friends and followers and provides another boost to community awareness.

One final cross-channel trick worth mentioning is a chat-to-community integration that some vendors offer. In this scenario before a customer enters a chat session, the community is searched to see if the answer to their issue already exists. If so, the customer can avoid a one-on-one session, greatly reducing support costs. Equally at any time, customers can escalate from community support to chat support with a click of a button. Neat!

However, while all this is technically possible and indeed boasts some examples it remains an unexploited opportunity. As a guess, one of the reasons is that community managers are in truth silo bound and therefore unlikely to be charged with running the other social channels. This is fine providing someone else is thinking more broadly in ecosystem terms. Otherwise this is a missed opportunity and to our way of thinking is further reason for developing and sharing an umbrella strategy which catalyzes greater uptake of these types of cross-channel opportunities.

The benefits of peer-to-peer support

So now we have covered why they work and how they fit in, let's discuss why they matter. As far as mainstream support is concerned, the consensus is that when communities gain enough momentum, they can remove between 10 and 20% of contact centre traffic. Obviously, this can be a huge benefit for organizations with large customer bases. According to ComBlu's research this starts to kick in once 80%+ of the support content is generated by peers rather than brands' FTEs.

Michael Maoz, a VP distinguished analyst from Gartner, notes in a 2012 blog post that having observed four of these communities in action for a period of 12 months. His findings were as follows:

- On average over 40% of customers resolve their issues in the online community.
- This equated to an overall reduction of 15%+ of all service cases.
- The average ROI was 100% within 15 months.

Some communities have even more impressive stats. Nico Henderijckx, Sony's European Forums Communities Manager, achieves an 85% solve rate with peer-to-peer online support. He manages to do this by employing just 12 moderators for a community of over 1,000,000 consumers across Europe. Both he and Jerome Pineau (ex Autodesk) also report that complex problems are solved faster by the community than via their contact centres.

These examples provide a pretty good indication of the current benefits on offer. A larger list of achievements is provided below. Moreover, as far as we are aware, this is the only form of Social Customer Service that has so far managed to articulate commercial benefits that would resonate with a financially minded executive. One good reason therefore to build your foundation on proven ROI. However, there is another absolutely key benefit that needs spelling out.

Peer-to-peer communities are the best way to scale social support!

In the context of this book's main theme, this is the primary and transformative benefit of peer-to-peer support. Here is the logic for this claim.

While current levels of social customer enquiry are not yet massive, they have to be anticipated as a likely outcome in a world going digital and social. Building a Social Customer Service capability entirely around staffing social network demand takes social strategists down the same path as their call centre brethren.

If they do that, those teams will no doubt suffer similar optimization ploys; from ill thought through outsourcing to untenable expectations for self service in an effort to reduce people costs. In the process, quality will be compromised. Customers will hate it. So will advisors. Brands will suffer. So let's not go there!

Instead, peer-to-peer support should be the backbone of your Social Customer Service strategy. In this context your presence on social networks becomes secondary. They provide outreach for customers but are in reality integrated extensions of the peer-to-peer support community in terms of how they operate and seek to build community membership. It is well understood that as community use grows, costs are nowhere near proportionate. giffgaff manages a customer base in excess of 300,000 with just 14 employees. Each community will have its own version of that cost benefit.

"I've seen organisations take 10% of their call volume onto social and self-service which takes about 8 people to handle. The other 250 people were handling the other 60,000 calls, emails and chats on a 1:1 basis."

Michael Pace – Head of Customer Care and Cultivation,

PerkStreet Financial

One of the key benefits of an integrated service strategy, a theme threaded throughout this book, is that operational decision making remains joined up. In this example, it means those who run Twitter and Facebook do not immediately increase resources as demand scales. Instead they work with the community management team to leverage community knowledge in order to divert demand. They also link to it wherever possible in order to transition customers over time to the community habit.

Some brands offer a simple dialogue box that sends the question straight through to the community. In the case of BTs UK Facebook, the whole of the community home page is made available with links into YouTube self-help clearly visible as well.

Of course not all customers will do cross-channel. Some will always prefer the ambience of their preferred channel. We still write and send letters to some customers! But in terms of strategy, the aim is to match customer demand with peer expertise and therefore produce a scalable and affordable support model.

Examples of peer-to-peer support

So, who is worth learning from? Happily there is a wealth of case studies. Platforms vendors cultivate these examples and a few run their own awards to incentivize the sharing of benefits. These are a few examples of what has been achieved:

Mint.com – consumer financial management software

In the first 90 days, the company saw a 75% reduction in the number of support tickets, saw 50% of traffic arrive via SEO and engaged 90,000 registered users across 15,000 topics; customers have also generated 2,965 ideas.

giffgaff – SIM mobile provider

Average response time for questions is within just three minutes (24/7). Telefonica (their owners) estimate giffgaff's Customer Service model costs 4 times less than the traditional contact centre-centric model. Their NPS score is 75 – way above the industry average and rivals Google and Apple. In terms of additional engagement they have received over 8,000 ideas from customer over a three-year period with 250 of them being implemented.

Citrix – server and desktop virtualization

Achieved 15% reduction in call centre traffic within the first month, thereafter stabilizing at 30%.

Tomtom – navigational software

20,000 cases handled and £150,000 payback within the first two weeks following launch. 25,000 page views and 150 new registrations a day.

Lenovo – laptop manufacturer

Moderators are all customer volunteers from around the world. 30 members have contributed 44% of the solutions over the last three years. There has been a 20% reduction in call volumes

SAP – enterprise software

2 million internal and external members who generate 6,000 posts every day and over 2,000,000 service assets including posts, blogs, wikis, whitepapers.

Linksys – hardware

£20m saved though call deflection.

Hewlett Packard – software

Customer satisfaction scores improved by 15%.

BT – Triple play provider

Cost savings after four months totalled £122,000 in terms of call deflection.

PDI – Back Office software

They reduced inbound support calls by 10% by targeting customers with the highest support calls and transitioning them to 24x7 community support. Within two months of launch, customers had shared 60–70 best practices the company had never thought of.

The outlook for peer-to-peer support

The future for peer-to-peer support looks bright. All the evidence suggests that it is possible to develop successful online communities for most types of organization embedded into any technology ecosystem. Do however, bear in mind this observation from Bian Salins:

> "Is there the need for an *immediate* answer. Will your customers wait for an answer to emerge from the community? If not, they may prefer Live Chat rather than peer-to-peer support."

We end this chapter with a few trends that are set to keep the peer-to-peer support market vibrant. Let's start with a "big" one; the transformative task of becoming a social business. Many advocates of the social business model see external/internal collaboration as central to their mission of building next generation organizations.

The core lessons that communities teach – listening, light touch facilitation, omni-directional leadership and outcomes based activity – are all "must have" behaviours in this context. So in organizations yet to sample community engagement, Customer Services could provide leadership by being the first to embrace a customer community.

The next trend flows out of the first one. Peer-to-peer support platforms have a close affinity with collaboration platforms. Jive for instance boasts a single platform for both external and internal collaboration which facilitates the natural flow of interaction between those that ask and those that can answer.

Other solutions also integrate with the most common collaboration platforms and can push conversations directly into a user's activity stream. This then provides enterprise-wide exposure to community conversations and raises awareness of customer issues. In terms of outcomes it also brings a broader range of expertise to fix issues. Particularly when they are complex or are less commonly understood issues.

This strategy of involving a wider range of employees than just full time support teams is an idea whose time is coming. "Everyone is responsible for customer service." This idea will be familiar to anyone schooled in systems thinking.

For instance, Best Buy is known to have trained and mentored an additional 2,000 employees to answer questions sent to its Twitter based service called Twelpforce. Dell opted to train 5,000 of its employees to directly engage with customers with a further 2,000 certified by Dell University.

Some have approached this internal recruitment in a more incremental way. While he was Autodesk's social media strategist, Jerome Pineau, shared the following idea on his blog while discussing how his organization approached ROI for social support:

"One interesting metric is the size of what we call our 'network map' – a dynamic internal system we created to tally social service 'contact points' throughout the company as we encounter them. The thicker, wider that network graph gets, the more efficient your social business gets."

In other words, part of Jerome's strategy was to progressively enrol others to collaborate in the Social Customer Service mission.

The last trend we are going to explore is what's new in the world of peer motivation. This is an important topic since it is what fuels the community dynamic and produces those amazing examples we covered earlier in the chapter.

While it is generally recognized that neither users nor super users do what they do for the money, there needs to be payback for their effort. Hence the notion of being awarded kudos (praise) for helping out and having that as part of one's community profile is a well established tactic and works well.

On top of that are other tokens of recognition to reward the super user. These can range from being granted access to private spaces on the community for briefings with the community management team (Virgin Media) to pre-release access to new products (Sony). Sometimes community managers will even fund paid for visits to the organization for extra training and meetings. For instance Nico Henderijckx invests 40% of his budget on bi-annual all expenses paid super user conferences to boost skills and allow super users and company executives to rub shoulders.

giffgaff also pays out. "Payback Points" are awarded every six months. These points are accumulated for referring people to the service, helping people by answering specific questions and solving technical issues in the community. The points can then be applied against their monthly mobile services, taken as a cash reward, or donated to a charitable cause.

Adding further momentum to all of this is the arrival of Gamification. From a technical perspective this allows you to reward specific behaviours such as creating, commenting and replying to topics. Gamification platforms typically use a variety of recognition tools from badges, to leaderboards to redeemable points.

How does this contribute to existing methods? Gamification exploits the lessons learned from the games industry, which as every parent knows, excels at persuading users to keep on playing. If this translates into community benefit, then maybe it will finally change the 90.9.1 run by encouraging more people to actively participate in helping out, thus raising average levels of responsiveness.

It might also deliver on a broader engagement agenda and help migrate the customer who originally arrived to get an issue fixed into a regular participant, now sharing thoughts via blog posts, building collaborative information in wikis, uploading documents, photos and videos.

In other words, Gamification within a support community context could help push an organization further down the road to a full social business model.

Tips

- If you want to build community, be prepared to hear from them.
- Never put your super users down in public.
- If you listen to their feedback, act on it and build the relationship and trust; there are super users out there that are willing to spend 40–45 hours a week on the community.
- Don't promise your super users anything that you might fail to deliver.

Thanks to Bian Salins for inspiring these tips.

Here is a final inspiring example of what can happen when you get your customers involved.

Barclaycard tapped the power of the crowd (their card members) to collaborate on building a better credit card experience. They launched a community where card members could exchange ideas, vote on product features and earn "credits" for their participation. The result is Barclaycard Ring, the world's first community designed credit card. Because the offering was designed by its users instead of a business unit, it launched with unprecedented features, an enormous differentiator.

Why Internal Collaboration Matters

Cormac Connolly is Director of Channel Development at Virgin Media.

Virgin Media is the first provider of all four broadband, TV, mobile phone and home phone services in the UK, offering a variety of entertainment and communications services to millions of residential and commercial customers across the country. Cormac leads the development of the evolving non-voice channels across self service, social, forums, chat, video and apps as part of delivering on Virgin Media's commitment to provide a choice of contact channels to their customers.

When did you get into Social Customer Service at Virgin Media?

While we had previously dabbled with social media, 2011 was the year our social strategy really took off and that's when I became more involved with the channel. We faced all the usual challenges that companies come across with social and at first, it felt like dipping our toes in the water without knowing if piranha were waiting to bite! In the beginning, we had a fairly ad-hoc approach to managing inter-actions that wasn't completely aligned within our existing customer management channel strategy. We weren't sure if we even needed to do it and were very aware of the risks of getting involved with it.

What made you bite the bullet?

I could definitely see there was a customer appetite for social and particularly as we're a broadband provider there was an expectation we would service this channel. Our first challenge was to get a more structured approach in place; I wanted to start including social along-side self service and the other non-voice channels and integrate it into our overall customer management channel strategy. My key aim was to develop an approach that simultaneously covered service while encouraging customer advocacy.

Did you need to convince people internally?

When we started focusing on the development of the social media channel, the executive director of customer care was relatively new to the organization and was very supportive and passionate about social. We didn't have a real plan of what we were going to do, but did have a vision of what we wanted to achieve and that was to manage interactions as effectively as possible and make people feel that we were actually listening and responding to them. We felt that the best way to manage interactions was through the customers' chosen non-voice channel and we would only take the customer offline when necessary.

Did you have a formal strategy and policies?

We just started off with a couple of written aspirations and guidelines and a small team. My steer to everybody was "let's go as fast as we can but as slow as we need to go". I wanted to make sure that we were in as much control of what was happening as we could be, as I didn't want to over-promise and under-deliver. We also had multiple stakeholders to engage with across the organization and needed to take them on the journey with us in a collaborative way.

What resources and tools did you need?

We continued to learn as we went along and gradually built up our resources as and when we needed them, starting off with a very basic tool for managing our social interactions. As demand grew, I appointed somebody in my team to be specifically responsible for assisted service as a channel. Having someone who literally lived and breathed assisted service and got stakeholders engaged across the organization was a real turning point. We now have around 30 people in the social customer care team and although that is a small allocation of the overall advisor community, I expect it will continue to grow and we re-forecast every three months.

We currently have over 66,000 Twitter followers and 221,000 customers connecting with us on Facebook and the team deals with about 800 tweets and 150 Facebook posts a day. The more customers see that we are responding to them in those channels the more that are using it. Some customers now use that as their channel of choice, which is quite interesting as they almost know the people in the social media team. As a result of this, we have invested in improved operational systems to cover workflow management as the team and operational needs have grown.

How have you structured those teams?

At the moment I keep the roles in the non-voice channels separate to voice so people can come and experience working in that environment. We've recruited internally, externally and from other departments and look at a slightly different skill set for people we bring onto these teams. We look for creative people who have a spark that shows that they are not afraid to let part of themselves to come to life in the conversation. The nature of the role means they have to put themselves on display a little bit, so they can't be afraid of that.

How have you trained the teams?

We train them by using practical examples and set the guidelines without getting prescriptive. We typically ask "If this was a Tweet that you saw, how would you answer it?" We're not necessarily looking for the cleverest answer; we're more interested in someone's ability to read the mood of the customer. We also value good grammar and spelling – we'd rather have a well written functional tweet than a funny one that is full of grammatical or spelling errors.

Do you develop people into the social team?

As we bring people into the social channel it follows a different induction programme to our voice agents. With the voice channel, there is a huge amount to learn about the systems to be effective from day one. New starters in the social channel can respond to simple tweets initially, or we can give them a certain number of links that they can signpost to and then over a period of time we bring them through that system training. They are effective earlier, and it makes it a little bit less intimidating than spending four or five weeks in a classroom before they can take their first phone call. For longer term development, people move around between different functions and roles and we benefit from some cross-skilling between voice and non-voice channels. They are all core Customer Service functions and there is no hierarchy between them. People self-select as to where they'd like to be.

What are the views at Virgin Media on One Agenda?

We took the lead on social from our customer care teams and I firmly believe this was the right decision for Virgin Media. In many cases, social tends to be led by marketing and while that's absolutely valid and fine for some companies, others are better driven from a care and a customer management perspective. Of course, you absolutely have to have all your stakeholders engaged and onboard with what you're doing.

How did you achieve that in practice?

We worked very closely with a number of stakeholders across the business to get them on board and there was no sense of "we own social" or "you own social". It is seen as just a channel and we all have to get the most out of it depending on whatever our needs are. Of course, there will always be some things that cause clashes here and there but we've always worked through them and have got to a really healthy balance across customer care, marketing and PR. Looking back, I would say we got there without making that a deliberate goal, rather an engaging approach and that's the way it played out.

What is the "voice" style of your brand through social?

The brand that we have lets us communicate in quite an edgy way sometimes, so we can balance being a little bit cheeky with being sympathetic at the same time. I find it incredible to see customers who are completely hacked off with us turned around by a bit of clever human intervention from a social agent. I think one of the main elements that has fascinated me about the social channel is the emotional interaction you have with that customer, it is completely unique compared to other channels. If similar comments were made in a call or email customers might find them strange or hard to accept, whereas in social they just take them at face value.

Can you give us an example?

Our social agents are always looking to creatively engage customers, drive advocacy and raise awareness of our brand. For example, one customer recently tweeted that he'd just opened the door to our broadband engineer wearing just a towel. It wasn't even a service query, but one of the guys in the social team spotted an opportunity for a bit of fun and tweeted back with "Did the technician look after your equipment ok?" The customer tweeted that he thought our response was really funny and then a couple of his followers came back to say that the comment had made their day. This is just one example of an interaction that we didn't necessarily need to acknowledge, but made a big impact on customer advocacy by giving a fun, human response.

Another thing to consider is that a number of high profile people use our services. If they tweet something about us, they can be very influential because they usually have a significant number of followers. If what they say is positive it can be hugely powerful, but if it's negative it can be very damaging; that's the power of a social service centre and why it needs to be managed so carefully.

So how do you manage it carefully?

Our advisors work within set guidelines but we mainly leave it to them to decide how they respond to interactions. It's simply not possible to respond to every single interaction, so our agents have to be selective and as a result of this Service and Sales queries often get priority. However, over and above this it's pretty much up to them and we really encourage them to bring their personalities into their responses.

Does a social crisis not scare you?

We haven't responded incorrectly yet, but we are big enough to know that one day it might happen. We've got a "response plan" in place which contains a set of quick steps about what to do if something were to happen in the social space. The plan has a key list of stakeholders to contact in an emergency and how to formulate the response quickly etc. The timeline between the issue arising and the need to mitigate it is very short. It's like any disaster recovery process; you can't have five meetings to work out what has happened. You can't go silent. You must be ready to say "we got it wrong" and "we're trying to put it right" and take action fast.

Do you think social has deflected calls or have you invited contact that you wouldn't otherwise have had?

It's a difficult one to factually prove or disprove, and you have to look a little more holistically at what you achieve in this channel. As a rule of thumb, about 5% of complaints are being handled through social which would have come through voice and email.

It's inevitable some of the contacts may not have ended up in voice or email but equally, we can't specifically measure the deflection of posts which end up being useful to other customers. For example, some customers might experience a problem with their connection but solve it themselves after looking at previous posts and tweets about re-setting their router.

Can you demonstrate ROI on social?

I'd confidently say it is at least on par to serve in social than serve in voice. Over time, I hope to prove the total benefit by evaluating not just call deflection but also customer advocacy and acquisition. We deliberately didn't spend a lot of time proving the business case, we just got on with it knowing it's a channel we have to service in a cost effective way. We have gradually migrated agents from voice to non-voice channels including social without overall incremental headcount and have not had any detrimental impact on service levels. We believe that a big part of our future is about our customers advocating our services based on their social interactions with us.

How do you convince people it's not optional?

Telephoning and emailing is becoming alien to the younger generation. Sometimes parents can only get in touch with their kids through Facebook! We just knew that our customers want to interact with us that way. If you don't listen, you don't know what people are saying about you as an organization.

What are the next steps in your aspirations?

I certainly see the social team becoming a more multi-skilled team and resource will gradually blend across the non-voice channels in time. A next step will be to develop into communities, forums, chat and video support, which will be a challenge to integrate as some people prefer calls when you take them offline while others want to follow-up on email. We try to use the customer's preferred channel while operating in a cost effective way.

What are your final tips for our readers?

You can't answer everything – the best approach is to manage a key number of interactions in influential places. Trying to respond to every interaction will only spread resources thinly and set the unrealistic expectation that every mention of a brand online will get a response. In our case, that certainly isn't realistic – we want to walk before we can run. We are interacting on Twitter, Facebook and our own website. We have good service levels in terms of response times and I'd rather improve that even further than be less effective over multiple social spaces. Finally, be open to learn and change as you go. It's not as scary as you might think; it's just another place where customers go when they need help.

Chapter 6

How to Use Facebook for Social Customer Service

Facebook celebrates its 10th birthday on 4 February 2014. At the time of writing, more than one billion people "like" and comment on Facebook posts at an average rate of 3.2 billion times every day. Those billion people have also made over a trillion connections between themselves. 58% of them can be classified as daily active users. No surprise then that Facebook is the 800-pound gorilla of social engagement.

Given those stats, many organizations naturally conclude that a substantial percentage of their own customers are on Facebook. True for large and small, as for B2C or B2B. Thus they busy themselves promoting, entertaining and otherwise trying to engage people to become fans. Once achieved, they win the right to become part of a fan's daily newsfeed and then compete along with family and friends for that person's attention and interest.

It is of course this opportunity to appear in the inboxes of family and friends that makes Facebook Customer Service so consequential. Your brand equity might rise a smidgeon if you are noticed doing something right to a mate or a sibling. Equally you might suffer a verbal lashing if a friend is seen to be in need over an unresolved service issue. Or maybe neither happens. A friend's holiday photos have captured all the attention. You really can't predict who will be influenced by the impact of your service capabilities.

Meanwhile back on your fan page, social marketing is cranking the wheel and filling up the timeline to maintain engagement levels. This is where the "happy" stuff happens. Fans comment and visitors are drawn in to become fans. If the stream of "stuff" hits the spot, people return and create a degree of community around what gets discussed.

However, that agenda is, at best, a shared one between what the social marketing team puts out and what the fans and visitors decide to talk about. And if Customer Service issues need discussing, they will appear. As luck would have it, probably right next to a "happy" item, maybe provoking an already angry customer even more.

What distinguishes Facebook from Twitter as a service environment is its increased visual impact. From the ease of scrolling its timeline to the redesigned, more graphic orientated inbox. This affects how service issues are experienced.

As part of researching this chapter, we looked at a range of fan pages to connect with real customers and real issues. Supermarkets and airlines had particularly vocal customers. Maybe it's just the nature of their products and services that excites more extreme concerns. Let's take the supermarket example to make the point about impact.

A combination of late deliveries, poorly packed and out of date food had provoked a post that was equal in length to a decent blog and carried a headline image of a bag of mouldy grapes. The author was a mother concerned about her next week's packed school lunches, a scenario that would resonate with many who had already zoned in on her post.

Another post, showing a half-eaten pasty with bits of bone scattering a tabletop, convinced us not to shop there again. At least not until new leadership at that particular retailer takes control. Moving up and down the timeline, it was clear these were not uncommon examples.

Free from any word count restriction combined with the visual ability to embed "forensic" evidence, these irate customers can make their case in a uniquely powerful way. Moreover this is now easily done via their smartphone camera and a Facebook app which already accounts for 60% of Facebook traffic. "Customer-as-detective with mobile crime lab" is the new reality.

So what are the lessons here and does this influence the way Customer Service should be organized on Facebook?

First of all, there is nothing new about organizations having issues and dealing with them. That is why we have Customer Service teams, return policies etc. However, the way in which these issues now run side by side with promotional and branding activity is new. Does this matter? No doubt the research into how this impacts consumer sentiment will arrive soon enough to tell us. Meanwhile let's draw our own conclusions. This is the core issue as we see it.

Although we might know that a brand provides appalling Customer Service via its call centres we still happily buy from them. Those two realities can be divorced in our experience. However, what happens when both the "offer to buy" and the "evidence we should not buy" appear in the same context, next to each other? We already know that customers trust friends, family and other consumer opinion ahead of branded messaging.

And to pour more oil on the fire, it is reasonable to assume that the "customer-as-detective with mobile crime lab" is now even more likely to voice her opinion, given how easy it is to do and the audience-as-witness she knows is at hand. In fact, some US retail brands now report how some customers check into their social service channels daily.

Add all that together and our conclusion is that all forms of Customer Service now have to be plugged into both a "fix it now" workflow and an "eliminate the cause of the issue" workflow. Otherwise you are killing your brand in public.

This conclusion affects your Facebook (and overall social support) strategy as follows. For sure, responsiveness matters; so invest in a suitable moderation and workflow solution that assigns tickets, has interaction history capability, CRM integration and all the rest of the functionality required to stay on the ball. Equally, invest in skilled resource able to respond authentically yet still avoid getting the brand stung when a swarm suddenly arrives to buzz angrily about a topic.

But none of this is sufficient. Right at the top of your agenda has to be discussion and decisions amongst the senior team about how they intend to plug their own intervention into the "eliminate the cause of the issue" workflow. This will be counter culture to many organizations. In the old days of purely private support interactions, the sight of customer issues could be removed from top table agendas and delegated to the next level of operational management. However, Social Customer Service re-amplifies those issues by revealing their causes. These are often strategic in nature and do require senior intervention.

For instance, the most common themes that can be currently witnessed on the Facebook pages of UK retailers are supply chain and delivery problems. In some cases, they even appear fundamental. Have a look for yourself. This is the point; everyone else is, including competitors. And by the way, each industry has its own version. Yours included.

The point we want to drive home is that the causes of repetitive service issues need to be fixed rather than tolerated. However, incredible the flair of your Social Customer Service, it is still only band aid. And once reviewed and fixed, something new will take their place. It never ends. It's called managing a business. Only this time, the world and his dog see the raw evidence before it is even compiled into the next board report.

You are being watched in real-time. But the answer is not to delete comments or keep your Facebook closed to comment as some organizations still instinctively try to do. They will always appear somewhere else. That much is certain. Much better to listen, learn and improve. In the end it is the only way to maintain a brand's dignity!

So, having triple emphasized the importance of getting an improvement culture in place, facilitated by appropriate senior intervention, let's return to the issue of responsiveness and the options for delivering Facebook Customer Service.

Not so long ago, brands were doing a pretty poor job in terms of recognizing and responding to service related topics being posted on Facebook. Many commentaries pegged responsiveness as low as 30%. Mercifully, things are improving. Social Bakers, one of the monitoring firms that has zoned in on this issue, have developed their own ongoing metrics and league tables. Just search for "Socially Devoted" to find the latest results on who are the current pacesetters and laggards. By the way these sorts of league tables are bound to multiply and enter into mainstream consumer consciousness.

At the time of writing, Social Bakers' analysis, was that "percentage answered" had leapt from 30% to 55% between Q2 and Q4 2012, while "time to answer" had improved from 20.9 hours to 13.7 hours in the same time period. This was based on a global sample of over a million organizations' Facebook properties. These improvements are an encouraging trend that hopefully reflects a young industry now maturing quickly.

Of course these SLAs (service level agreements) are averages and only indicate that an overall improvement is taking place. It is worth bearing in mind that in a 24 × 7 culture, this global benchmark gets dragged down when service teams sign off end of day/end of week. Also territories such as the US suffer from time zone lags which can compound responsiveness issues unless effective resourcing strategies are put in place.

So given those improvements are we now hitting target? Unfortunately the research suggests organizations are still chasing customer expectations. According to a 2012 study from NM Incite, a joint venture between Nielsen and McKinsey & Company, 83% of Twitter users and 71% of Facebook users now expect a Customer Service response from a brand within a day. Incidentally more than 50% of Twitter users expect a response within two hours.

Whether your own customers expect even better all depends. As an airline responding to customers trying to catch a flight, clearly you need to be much more responsive than 13.7 hours. KLM get that and reportedly deliver a 26-minute average first response time and a 92% post response rate to questions asked on Facebook.

What about if you are a retailer needing to recover a delivery failure so that the new party frock arrives in time for that all important Saturday night out? This again demands you are fast enough if you intend to win kudos for saving the day and want to see that being posted into your potential customers' inboxes. That is if you are pursuing a "Service Is The New Marketing" strategy.

By the way the same study also concluded that customers who receive a quick and effective response are three times (71%) more likely to recommend the brand, compared to just 19% who will still recommend the brand if they don't receive a response.

So now you know what it's going to take to look good in front of your fan's family and friends.

Setting up and operating Facebook as a customer service facility

Assuming you have decided to respond to customers' service needs on Facebook, what needs thinking through? Let's start with strategy and then move onto operational matters.

This starts for multi-national organizations with the question of how best to set up their Facebook presence. The confusion caused by multiple territories and functions all setting up/abandoning their own Facebook pages without any central co-ordination has only just been overcome. So organizations are naturally keen to stay in control. What are their options currently?

Assuming you have a need, Facebook allows you to organize your presence locally and globally. The most common approach to date has been to offer local pages, most often at country level. However, in 2012 Facebook introduced a new option in the form of global pages. Note that these are only for organizations that "work directly with Facebook" (i.e. invest campaign budget with Facebook). Users who visit a global page are automatically directed to the version specific to their region, but they can still access any regional or global page through a drop-down menu.

This is a good example of where Marketing and Customer Service should have detailed understanding of each other's needs and plans since they are sharing a common platform. Reported uptake does suggest that a global page strategy helps simplify some of the complexities around managing Facebook marketing activity.

But the question for Customer Service leaders is how does this fit in with their existing service strategies around resourcing and infrastructure? There may be multi-lingual resourcing implications. Or non-integrated Customer Service infrastructure between regions. These need articulating and discussing before decisions around the "common good" can be made. Even though this will only come up as an occasional issue, it still matters especially in Marketing led social support teams who might not be as aware of service priorities.

Of course there could be an even simpler approach. Serif, a software publisher, has split Marketing and Support for both Facebook and Twitter. While this is increasingly common for Twitter, Facebook homepages are still usually shared. You can read the full interview with Alex Loach, Serif's Head of Service Operations, at the end this chapter and how this has worked out.

Once the approach to localization is established, the next strategic issue is deciding the functionality you intend to offer via your Facebook page. This question takes you into the heart of your overall service strategy in terms of how you view the value of Facebook within your overall service mix.

As we have said elsewhere neither Facebook nor Twitter are ideal Customer Service environments out of the box. But they can certainly be made fit for purpose.

To start with, make sure you have an effective listening and issue allocation process from a service perspective. For instance if Marketing is still in pole position in terms of running Facebook, many of their preferred social media marketing platforms, such as Buddy Media, Context Optional or Wildfire, offer moderation features that allow Customer Service teams to be pinged and prompted to respond. However, this is not ideal. No-one is really minding the shop from a service perspective in this scenario.

So make sure you resource with either a dedicated service team or a hybrid Marketing/Service team to maintain responsiveness. Secondly make sure that the listening process is "tuned" to service needs as we have mentioned previously. Finally, choose a platform that is specifically designed for Customer Service This could be one of "pure plays" such as Conversocial and Brand Embassy or veteran vendors such as Genesys and Aspect who have extended into social channels. The various issues that surround this decision are explored in Chapter 4 question 4.

This will then advance you to the point of being able to efficiently respond to your fans' service issues. This is the milestone which many organizations have currently reached. However, there is still a journey before you should consider yourself having an optimized presence on Facebook.

For a start, there remains this ongoing clash between brand messaging and service issues. If the answer is to use separate accounts on Twitter, what is the equivalent tactic for Facebook?

This is where the creative use of page tabs comes in. These sit at the top of your home page and can provide a way of diverting service issues into dedicated areas. The most common service tabs you are likely to see are Twitter, YouTube and access to peer-to-peer resources from the likes of Lithium, Parature and Get Satisfaction.

However, it is worth understanding a little more about how these work to appreciate the full potential that Facebook makes available to page administrators. In the admin dashboard, Facebook provides certain core apps such the ability to embed video, pictures, text and even run events.

For instance the text app could be used to build an FAQ while the event app could be used to promote live Q&A sessions with product experts. Something peer-to-peer support sites increasingly offer to boost member engagement.

However, in addition to these pre-integrated apps, Facebook also allows you to import third party apps in a similar way that a peer-to-peer platform allows you to extend functionality into social networks. This means you can join up the dots in the Customer Service journey from both directions.

Before going through any examples, we first need to put some context around the ones we sourced via the Facebook app directory site appbistro. com. Although we quote the name of each app and provide a brief description of how it could be used, this is in order to fire up your imagination and allow you to easily track them down if you then want to see screenshots.

In doing so, we are not verifying that they work. Nor do we assume that your own IT strategy would necessarily allow this form of integration. What we are suggesting though is that they show the art of the possible and that if the functionality strikes you as a "must have", then it is likely that with the proper due diligence you can either acquire it off the shelf or have it recoded.

The key point is that they allow you to customize Facebook into a powerful service ecosystem in its own right. This should appeal to both advocates of cross-channel design and also those who are heavily Facebook-centric as an organization.

Let's start with options to add extra interaction channels:

- **VeriShow** offers live chat, video conferencing and real-time content sharing. This could be an elegant way of transitioning a customer into a private "one to one". E-commerce customers are increasingly familiar with Chat. Interestingly Frank Eliason has integrated chat into @askciti Twitter feed so that customers can continue interacting with the same advisor.
- **Textingly** enables text messaging which remains the most popular form of consumer communication. Once this form of connection with a customer is made, both service issue updates and satisfaction surveys could be pushed to them.
- **Video Channel** allows you to integrate an entire You Tube channel. This means you could present your entire video self-help catalogue. The same effect could be achieved via a Pinterest board. See below.
- **Get Satisfaction** introduces the peer-to-peer channel. This allows a Facebook user to ask questions of that organization's peer-to-peer support community. Additionally they can share ideas, request a service ticket, even give praise. Another service function this integration intro-

duces is the ability to search for answers across sources of organiza-tional knowledge. This is not possible on a Facebook homepage despite holding potentially useful answers from other customer enquiries.

Having explored channel options, let's now look at additional informa-tion options that are useful for driving service agendas:

- **Livestream** allows you to broadcast live web events to mobile devices. Imagine using this as part of a new product launch educating users on new features to pre-empt service requests.
- **Slideshare** allows you to import presentations. These could be product guides in the form of e-books or indeed any form of instruction.
- **Mailchimp** allows you to add a mailing list signup form. This could provide a new service related communication channel between you and Facebook fans.
- **Newsletter** provides an email newsletter so that fans can keep track of new activity. This could be useful as part of your proactive support to reduce inbound volumes.
- **Staff Profiles** is a slightly different information app. It allows you to show individual profiles for the service team. This is sometimes used on Twitter service accounts to great effect as a way of creating a human connection.
- **Partner Page Promotions** showcases a list of partner pages. This could be used to link in any other organizations who can add value to service issues.

Finally, there are ways to connect Facebook into your Voice of The Cus-tomer activity:

- **Urtak Poll** allows fans to answer simple yes or no questions. This could be used as a simple way of gathering feedback on service quality. See Chapter 4 question 14.
- **UserVoice** is a feedback tool which allows customers to create, discuss, and vote for ideas. It also provides email alerts whenever someone

makes a new suggestion and/or comments. This could be used to provide the same capability as found on peer-to-peer platforms. Or it could be used to uncover priority customer issues as part of your drive to "eliminate the cause of the issue" workflow discussed at the start of this chapter.

If after all that, you still have an outstanding need to integrate service functionality via a page tab there is one remaining trick. This provides the key to pretty much any integration. It is an iframe technique which simply means any application functioning in a browser can do the same thing in a page tab.

This is how some Facebook brands with peer-to-peer support sites have gone further than just provide a search capability. Instead they deliberately offer access to the entire home page of their community via the tab. It is also the way in which to present an entire page of self-help videos via a Pinterest board. Or a support related blog. Or any service application you might want to offer to customers for that matter.

As a final brainstorming flourish, there is one more Facebook capability that could be used for service needs given some creative thought. As you probably know, Facebook is big on hosting games. This has proved a major hit and source of engagement. Which means the format is familiar to many. Organizations can build their own versions too. Access can be bookmarked on the homepage.

So given that existing momentum around the games format, why not adapt its use and build an interactive service resource built around product demos and service FAQs? It could be designed to house the most anticipated service requests and become a self service tool. Maybe this is something to consider for anyone wanting to differentiate their Facebook Customer Service.

That brings this chapter to a close. Remember the underlying point. Facebook and its third party app developers provide many options to extend service capability for users who are rooted to the format. In doing so it also provides connection paths to the rest of your Customer Service ecosystem for those that prefer or need to go cross-channel. Much of this extended capability is yet to be exploited by organizations.

Performance levels

While individual brand performances are likely to move over time, it is still worth being aware of real world performance standards. In Q4 2012 Brand Embassy tested Facebook responsiveness across major UK sectors. The following results represent the average level of responsiveness from each category leader after five enquiries.

Please note that this was just their initial speed to answer and does not judge the quality of their final answer or their ability to solve the issue. Also some brands were leaders by the smallest of margins. Nonetheless here are the numbers.

Brands that managed to respond within the half hour included Sainsbury and Toyota. Screwfix, ASOS and Vodafone all came back within the hour. Subway, Co-op and Sage managed the same task within two hours while Endsleigh took three hours. Maplin brought up the rear on behalf of electronic retailers with an eleven-hour average.

What does this tell us? For a start customers should expect quite different levels of responsiveness. Is this how fast each sector needs to be? This will be interesting to watch as the leaders in responsiveness set the pace. Will customers then expect similar standards?

Tips

We sign off this chapter with a series of operational tips:

- Respond to messages, don't delete them unless spam.
- Respond fast even if the answer takes longer.
- Be personal. You have the customer's name, use it. Let them know they're talking to a real person. It can positively modify a person's behaviour.
- Using canned responses undermines any sense that a real person is replying. So don't do it.
- Arguing with customers in public even when they have stepped over the line is a no-win outcome for you.
- Avoid legal style language such as "it appears that you . . .", when it is crystal clear in the customer's mind what has happened.
- Use private messaging when personal details need exchanging. Works for both fans and visitors. However, users do have to initiate this form of contact. Your side of the interaction will then appear in their inbox.
- Use "pinned" posts to highlight certain hot topics. They will then move to below the sharing tool in the top left of your Page's timeline, and an orange flag will appear in the upper-right corner.
- If you have to hand off a customer to mainstream Customer Service make sure you provide thorough briefing. Or then risk them reappearing later, much more frustrated.
- Fix issues. Allowing the same ones to keep reappearing suggests you are either not listening or nor really committed to helping customers.

Social as Part of Your Channel Mix

Alex Loach is Head of Service Operations for Serif; a developer and publisher of powerful, and easy-to-use software founded in 1987 with the aim to develop low-cost alternatives to high-end publishing and graphics packages. Serif's award-winning software is now used by more than 6.5 million customers worldwide and has over 250 employees at its head office in Nottingham.

How do you get started with Social Customer Service?
We had been using social for one-way marketing for some time but we started on the Social Customer Service journey by setting up Twitter first and then about six months later we set up a Service & Support Facebook page for Customer Service. We have also been using YouTube as a form of self-help.

What social channel was most effective for your brand?
We have probably found Facebook has been the better tool for us to deliver Customer Service through, largely because of the support we provide being technology information that can't be easily relayed in 140 characters. Our customers often want an instant and detailed answer and Facebook has been great for that.

The volumes across the various channels have been as follows:

	Calls	Emails	Chats	Social Media
2011	67%	32%	1%	1%
2012	59%	32%	1%	8%
2013	56%	31%	<1%	13%

These volumes demonstrate the effect that we believe social media has had on calls (with the telephone channel being the other option for an instant answer) rather than emails which tends to be used by those willing to wait for a response. For us, we estimate a call costs almost 8 times that of a social media interaction, so we can safely say we are realizing some efficiency savings. We notice that our customers from ten years ago are still contacting us through the telephone but our new customers seem to find us online and then want to interact with us online. As a technology company we naturally have a lot of tech-savvy customers.

How have you integrated social with your traditional channels?
We developed our more experienced advisors in what we wanted for social responses for a dedicated team. First we took one Customer Service advisor and trained them in social media and then slowly expanding that team. New starters begin on email, move to telephone and finally social. Because it is an open platform we view it as a bit of a knowledge base to our products so the information we put out there has to be right. The next question is how we integrate our community into our social media Customer Service.

What are your predictions for the next three years?
Our new generation of customers wants an increasingly fast response, so we have put resources into it to provide that. I think email correspondences won't be instant enough. 12 or 24 hours won't be quick enough. I think the demand for Social Customer Service is going to grow. You can't wait until you feel ready to offer it as an organization, it's demand led from customers. I think we have to offer all the channels and provide quality and quick responses with all the channels.

How do you manage social internally?
We had a debate in the early days as to which function was going to "own" social but we decided quite quickly to separate out the Marketing Facebook page and Twitter handle and then the Service & Support Facebook page and Twitter and this has worked well. We

probably get most crossover on Twitter but it's just a case of passing the tweets over from the corporate handle to the Customer Service handle.

We have guidelines and training for our advisors in place so that they know the company style and what is expected. However, we put a massive amount of effort to employ support advisors with personality and so we do try not to constrain that too much. We try to let them make their own decisions as much as possible. Occasionally they might make wrong decisions but that is the choice we make. If they do get it wrong then we take them to one side and discuss it. At times advisors have left us which has made me nervous and I've changed passwords very quickly but none of them did anything and they had the opportunity. I think if you get the caring, friendly people in the position in the first place then you are halfway there. Even for a technical support role like ours we are looking for warmth and trustworthiness.

What are your next steps with Social Customer Service?

We will be focusing on cultivating our community to assist with customer engagement and self-help. To date we have been very focused on providing quick Social Customer Service responses ourselves, but ironically, this has probably delayed the community involvement as we always got there first! We have been consciously holding back a little to allow the answers to come from the community and our forums. We will be providing a cool place for our customers to hang out online and cultivating that knowledge base for further self-help.

Chapter 7

How to Use Twitter as a Service Channel

On 21 March 2006, Jack Dorsey sent the first public tweet informing the rest of the world he was *"just setting up my twttr"*. Since then it has grown into a major communication platform. As of mid-2012, there were 170m active accounts globally and around 10m in the UK.

Just in case you have yet to join in, Twitter allows users to read and publish text messages of up to 140 characters ("tweets"). This keeps communication simple and reduces bandwidth issues. Tweets are publicly visible by default, but senders can restrict message delivery to just their followers. Users may subscribe to other users' tweets – this is known as *following* and subscribers are known as *"followers"*.

Pictures and video can also be attached but are not directly embedded within the body of the message as in a Facebook post. As the world trends towards more visual forms of communication Twitter has moved on with its own six-second video service called Vine. Yet its enduring simplicity is what makes Twitter uniquely interesting as a real-time barometer. Probably more so than any other social channel.

Interestingly the leadership team at Twitter prefer to brand themselves as a communication platform instead of being categorized as part of the social media space. They have a point. Twitter has carved out a very distinct niche for itself as an enabler of breaking news across the world. It's no secret that news agencies and governments tap into Twitter before any other source: the Japanese tsunami, global reaction to Usain Bolt winning gold, the death of Bin Laden. From news of global significance to matters just between a few local clubbers, there is always someone at hand ready to tweet what they have just witnessed.

And that's its beauty. Twitter is the ultimate example of crowdsourcing. In this case the news. What CNN achieved in providing 24 × 7 coverage, Twitter has taken forward and redefined what "real-time" now means. For instance, those who dabble in predictive analytics reckon that getting a forward position of stock movements is a possibility using real-time data mining of tweets. Time will tell.

How people use Twitter

Here are some key UK statistics that Twitter and Compete published as a joint research piece Q3 2012. As with Facebook use, we can see that Twitter is a mobile experience for most users enabling them to easily integrate it in their daily behaviour:

- 80% of UK users access Twitter via a mobile device.
- Mobile users are 40% more likely to access Twitter more than once a day.
- 1 in 3 use Twitter on their daily commute.
- 1 in 4 use Twitter while shopping.
- 67% follow brands on Twitter of which half follow for Customer Service.

To put some further context around level of brand interest, Topshop had racked up almost half a million Twitter followers by the start of 2013, making it the most followed retailer in the UK.

Think of Twitter as being the most successful experiment so far in a universal messaging service. That 140-character format keeps things simple. The speed at which tweets can go viral proves how easy it is for others to discover and amplify topics of interest. This is boosted by the common practice of spontaneously labelling an event and adding a hashtag to generate a real-time searchable topic. This allows others to quickly find, add to and pass on a common thread of discussion; the mechanics of how something goes viral.

Much of the fun of being on Twitter is participating in these global "Mexican waves". Analyzing a month's worth of viral tweets would show how diverse and random the topics are. Twitter incubates everything from the "Harlem Shuffle" to a story that your food product is suddenly contaminated with horsemeat. As with all forms of news service, Twitter can generate intense but fleeting attention.

The question for businesses though is what impact does it leave behind? For instance, how about being an airline losing a child during an internal flight and then appearing not to care that much? Red rag to a bull as it turned out for US carrier United Airlines in summer 2012!

Here is another example of how consumers can leverage its reputation when they feel an organization is not playing fair.

When my elderly father was fined for not having his payment card with his rail ticket, even though it was a reserved seat and he had many other means of providing his ID, the rail company would not refund the £120 extra pounds for his journey even when he wrote to them. I stepped in and threatened to use any means possible including twitter to highlight the unreasonable treatment and illogical reasons for the fine - suddenly we had vouchers to make up the extra fine. They do not want the bad publicity, people power.

- ██████ , England, 16/5/2012 12:46

Report abuse   Click to rate ⇧⇩ Rating ⬆ 10

Same with companies who have internet forums, so you can post your problems for the world to see. They probably provide VIP treatment because it's so open and easy for people to see. So if you don't get a satifactory resolution on the phone, just hang up then start the bad mouthing online and they will soon sort out your problems to a better resolution. A lot will give credit to account to seem like they are a company that likes to keep it's customers happy.

- ████ , Portsmouth, 16/5/2012 11:52

Report abuse   Click to rate ⇧⇩ Rating ⬆ 8

Evidence of this form of consumer activism is widespread. This form of behaviour is quickly learned and should be expected as part of the mindset of today's consumer. Here is advice from a certain social media consultant:

"Think about who might be interested in this story – prominent journalists, consumer advocacy groups, local politicians."

In fact, just as an experiment try this. Go to Twitter and type "poor Customer Service" into the search bar and just watch the continuous stream of angry sentiment scroll across your screen. What you are watching is the transitory, low level hum of customer upset when things go wrong. However, it is best to respect the fact that any one of them could turn into a Mexican wave.

"Sometimes it can go horribly wrong but most of it will be tomorrow's digital fish and chip-wrapping."
Maria McCann – Group Head of Customer Experience and Service for Aurora Fashions. Previously headed up Social Customer Service at Spotify and ASOS

However, Twitter also works beyond being a one-way announcement platform. Dialogue is possible. In fact live group discussions can work pretty well once you get the hang of it. You can check out some of these by searching for "tweetups", the slang for a live online session, which use hashtags such as #custserv to produce a kind of threaded conversation.

So against this background, it is no surprise that Twitter and Customer Service should come together. How did it actually happen? You could say both by accident and by design. The fact that customers escalate their issues via Twitter has led socially aware organizations to respond. In many cases by issuing specific Twitter handles (addresses) for service topics. This is the "deliberate" form of Social Customer Service via Twitter.

However, since a Customer Service issue is a form of personal news, it is natural that it can also end up just being tweeted. Maybe the Customer Service handle was not known, maybe the customer did not care and just wanted to let their social world know by adding in the brand name or brand product. This "accidental" stream of communication is increasingly tracked using a combination of social media monitoring tools augmented with human moderation.

Dell for instance, automates the process of scanning for the 22,000 daily instances they are referenced. As we know from our exploration of social monitoring in Chapter 4 question 3 those posts could be anything about Dell and not necessarily related to a Customer Service issue. But a growing proportion of them are. For instance a 2012 study of US retailers by Conversocial pegged the percentage of tweets that were service related at 37%.

When all sources of customer enquiry are effectively tracked, there can be mutual benefit for both customer and organization. While current adoption rates show that tweeting has yet to hit mainstream consumer awareness, it is a popular and effective form of communication for those in the know. Small issues can be solved in a simple tweet, and for more complex problems you can easily take the conversation to a direct message.

As the word gets out, expect more and more of your customers to convert to this form of initial interaction. Here is a personal example from Carolyn that shows how easily this conversion can take place.

"In April 2012 I had a problem with the water coming through the taps in my home. It was brown. I'm Generation X and for decades I have reached for the telephone to report such issues, but United Utilities are a training client of mine and I watch their social customer service channel with interest. So, going against the grain of my programming, I tweeted the following:

 @CarolynBlunt

@unitedutilities *hi we have got brown water coming thru taps this morning in PR5 4EH :(Any action needed to resolve pls???*

9:48 AM – 13 Apr 12 via Twitter for iPhone

While I was waiting I searched Twitter and immediately found the following from BBC Lancashire:

 BBC Lancashire@BBCLancashire

United Utilities is repairing a damaged valve, which has affected the water to 7000 homes in Bamber Bridge, Chorley and surrounding areas.

7:13 AM – 13 Apr 12via web

This reassured me that there was no point calling the United Utilities call centre. Approximately an hour after I had tweeted later I got a reply from United Utilities:

 United Utilities@unitedutilities

@CarolynBlunt *Sorry about this – engineers are flushing out the pipes. You can clear some sediment by gently trickling a downstairs tap.*

10:44 AM – 13 Apr 12via TweetDeck

I saved myself the time and effort of calling in. United Utilities saved themselves approximately £5 in telephone handling costs. Everyone was a winner in this situation."

Why some organizations won't get involved

In this instance the use of Twitter was risk free and a cost saving for the organization. If it is always this easy then why aren't more organizations leaping in to take advantage?

For some, the fear of reputational damage remains the issue. The transparency of social channels is risky and increases the chances that complaints become amplified and negativity towards the brand is allowed to grow. The not infrequent examples of brands that suffer a public drubbing on social channels only serve to reinforce this general reluctance. You may well be facing similar resistance in your own organization. However, contrast that with research headlines that kept appearing throughout 2012 which showed brands were ignoring up to 70% of service related tweets. Which is the more dangerous position to adopt?

The second issue is a more tangible concern: one of resourcing. Some organizations have been content to operate a 9–5 Twitter model and make that clear to their customers. Others though see an inevitable slide into 24x7 resourcing with all the logistical and cost implications that go with it. In other words, as customers' needs change so do their expectations. Some organizations are reluctant to catch up.

But whatever the internal considerations, the point to grasp and argue for is this. Twitter is often used as a service channel of last resort for customers. When phone, email and other channels fail, a desperate tweet is all that's left. The companies that are able to keep a customer from slipping through the cracks using Twitter have a great opportunity to redeem themselves. Others that ignore increase the odds of consumer activism and being "corporately mugged".

So the message here is a simple one to grasp. Social Customer Service via Twitter is fast becoming an expected norm. Ignore it at your peril. Moreover doing it really well is essential to encourage customers to leave positive commentary in your Twitter stream. Otherwise suffer whatever consequences this has on new customers warming up to your brand or existing customers wondering if the grass now looks greener elsewhere.

What's the business case for Twitter?

Those hoping to base their investment case on a simple cost reduction argument are in for a disappointment. Certainly there are stories that Twitter can solve customers' problems faster. Some of our interviewees are on record saying this is the case and as such can be referenced as part of your argument.

Yes faster does suggest that it should be a cheaper channel. But matters are not as clear cut as the argument for, let's say, peer-to-peer support, in which unpaid expert customers help other customers. Clearly cost benefit analysis in that model is easier.

The trouble here is that when you examine the customer's service journey that starts with a tweet, other channels are often quickly offered such as email, chat or phone. This muddies the water around working out the real "cost to serve".

Why is this happening? Some argue that the value of social interaction is by definition lost whenever it becomes private because others can no longer benefit. They also argue quite rightly that it is best practice to maintain the same channel throughout an interaction. They even frown on the use of direct messaging which is Twitter's version of going private. Others are more pragmatic. They say that the 140-character format is bound to cause cross-channel hopping. Others claim the sensitivity of customer information or the situation at hand demands privacy.

For whatever reasons, many have settled into a pattern of starting and ending an enquiry on Twitter with the middle section of case resolution being conducted in private. The cherry on the cake is if the customer leaves whatever praise they might offer in public as a parting gift.

If both parties are happy to work in this way, then the business case for Twitter is the same as for all new channels when they seek justification to become the latest member of a multi-channel strategy. Customers now expect it. This is seldom a strong financial argument in the short term, but it happens to be true.

So the business case needs to change tack and argue for *customer experience* benefits. Once a channel gains a reputation for being more convenient, your customers will start to demand it. In this case, convenience might be experienced as a genuinely more efficient way of getting something accomplished. Or it might mean that I just feel more attuned to certain communication channels, since that is my generation's way of doing things.

So getting the money for people and workflow that suits this type of Social Customer Service might not be straightforward. The elements you need to weave together are:

- The cost of reputational damage. From ongoing low level negative chatter to virally driven, one-off events.
- The removal of low complexity enquiries from the call centre queue that can be rapidly processed asynchronously.
- The upside benefits of being seen to help out a distressed customer when other channels have failed. Remember a customer with 7,000 Twitter followers commands a large audience.
- User-generated content is the advertising currency. It is so much more credible if a customer says you are great, as opposed to your own PR and Marketing team.

Twitter as part of your multi-channel strategy

Although this book is exclusively about social channels, you know by now that we are not suggesting they can or should replace existing customer channels. However, for those coming into the business of Customer Service for the first time via the social channel route, this might not be so obvious.

So here is the condensed primer on multi-channel strategy that has stood the test of time over the last twenty-five years.

1. Channels multiply rather than die

Across a typical customer-base that has a spread of demographics, some will prefer voice and some will prefer text. Some will feel more at home with one-to-one communication. Others will look for the benefits of a one-to-many style.

That means new channels seldom extinguish existing channels. For instance fax still hangs on as a transaction channel in certain B2B markets. Much as we might gripe about call centres, demand for live assistance over the phone remains anywhere from 40–70% according to multiple research sources.

Bottom line: *Best consider social channels as additions than replacements.*

2. There is no such thing as a "killer" channel

It is important to remind ourselves that every interaction channel has its strength and weakness. Twitter's 140-character format is both a strength and weakness depending on context. It's great for simple exchanges of ideas but severely limited for detailed discussion.

"The ones that get a kick out of nailing a message in 140 characters, they are the ones you want!"

Maria McCann – Group Head of Customer Experience and Service for Aurora Fashions. Previously headed up Social Customer Service at Spotify and ASOS

Also Twitter remains a confusing communication tool for those that do not use it regularly. This is why only a third of people who register their Twitter account remain active users. Its functionality is not intuitive and therefore has to be consciously learned; a big deterrent to the "pick it up and use it now" mindset. This is not to condemn Twitter outright since equivalent limitations exist with live voice, IVR, chat, Facebook, forums etc.

Bottom line: *Design to a channel's strengths rather than its weaknesses.*

With more than half of the UK now carrying smartphones, forecast to stabilize at around the 70% mark, the style of traditional Customer Service delivery is being transformed. Mobile Customer Service demands simplicity of operation. Whatever the latest generation of smartphone brings in terms of innovation, the reduced form factor (relative to a tablet or laptop) puts a premium on short, simple interaction.

This suddenly makes 140-character formats look more attractive. Especially if we consider that according to Twitter's own analysis, 80% of British tweets are made via mobile. Therefore most service enquiries will be made via a mobile device. In this context Twitter looks like a strong candidate for text based interaction. And until voice interfaces replace fat fingers on virtual keyboards, keeping descriptions to 140 characters will be a blessing. So Twitter's future as part of a multi-channel strategy, especially around mobile service delivery, looks assured.

The Twitter workflow

As part of set up you need to think through your overall Twitter activity. Foviance provided this useful distinction in a 2012 whitepaper on three different approaches.

Some organizations maintain a primary marketing focus yet recognize service issues and either provide contact details or pass them across to Customer Service teams. Examples are British Airways, First Direct, LOVEFiLM, OverheardAtMoo, PayPalUK.

Some just provide automated feeds for service announcements. Examples include MetOfficeUK, NationalRailEnq, NRE SWT, RedFerries.

Many brands however, have adopted the practice of adopting separate accounts for Marketing and Service. Examples include BTCare, ASOS HereToHelp, LloydsTSBOnline, LVCares, giffgaffHelp. ASOS has segmented even further and maintains separate feeds for men's and women's fashion.

Once you have that sorted out, then this is the typical workflow and associated competencies you need to be building and checking your progress against:

1. Effective responsiveness begins with tuning your monitoring platform. See Chapter 4 question 3 issues and tips for more guidance. Ensure that you scan for both @ and non @ mentions of your brand and key brand names. Identify most common language used by customers that indicates problems. Do the same for positive sentiment if it is your intention to reach out and acknowledge these as well.
2. The relevant posts are then picked out and forwarded for answering. The detail of what happens in this stage depends on the workflow tool you are using. Assuming you need something more sophisticated than

Google alerts and individuals picking off the tweets they personally feel drawn to responding to, your choices could include:

- A moderator's intervention to scan the tweet, possibly add a note and then allocate it.
- An automated queuing system that prioritizes based on definable rules, e.g. influencer score, # of followers, timestamp, interaction history etc.
- This is resourced either by a dedicated team for 140-character communication or a multi-skilled team in both Facebook and Twitter style communication.

3. Once allocated, individual tweets are then either responded to as a public threaded conversation or transferred to a private form of communication. This is driven by whatever policy you adopt on confidentiality and privacy. Customers have to be "following" you so you can direct message them and decide on how to proceed. That said, Twitter has allowed some brands to opt-in to receive DMs from accounts they don't follow, e.g. BTCare, ASOS HereToHelp, LloydsTSBOnline, LVCares, giffgaffHelp.

4. Options for following up after the direct message:
   - This could remain as the direct message format if the confidential matter is simple.
   - It could be live chat if the need is immediate and the 140-character restriction needs to be lifted.
   - It could be email if the need is less urgent.
   - It could be phone if the need is complex, emotive or is just a preferred channel for the customer.
   - Remember though, from a cross-channel perspective, it is highly desirable that the same person completes the interaction whichever channel is then chosen.

5. Once the matter is satisfactorily resolved, you should target some kind of customer recognition. Of course this cannot be forced. It is the litmus test of how well you have performed:
   - Check out @askciti for how they do it. Note the facility at the top of their Twitter feed that allows the full interaction to be shown or

hidden (Tweets All/No Replies). Do it well and the customer validations act as a powerful brand endorsement.
- If you have gone private and the customer is unlikely to return to give a public endorsement then consider this approach to gathering feedback.

TeamTurboTax @TeamTurboTax   1 Feb
@nicolematich Saw we helped on Twitter recently. Mind taking a moment for a short survey to tell us how we did? Thanks! tinyurl.com/aadngx3
Expand

---

6. In addition to the ongoing daily interactions, run some form of continuous improvement to keep the service improving:
   - Undertake regular quantitative and qualitative analysis of the topics you deal with on Twitter. Rank them. Identify those that can be answered as a text/video FAQ and make them available to the team. Use a url shortening service so you can track if they are subsequently used by other customers.
   - Reduce customer effort and decrease service costs by automating simple, high volume repeat activity. For instance, Virgin Atlantic provides an automated Twitter service. Tweet your flight number and departure information at it, and within seconds it spits back flight status information (thanks to Jerome Pineau for sharing this).
   - Poll customers on their reasons for using the service. For those that suffered a service failure via another channel collect the reasons and topics. Work with those service leaders to fix the issues. Getting them up to speed means you don't gain a reputation for being the only "sort it" channel in the Customer Service mix

In addition to this workflow which has hopefully given you a framework, here are a number of tips that have been gathered from an extensive trawl of all the best advice from real world practitioners.

Tips

1. Acknowledge quickly. Twitter is seen as an "instant" channel.
2. Proactively reach out on complaints even if not directly addressed to you.
3. Track the changing demand for SLAs as they move increasingly real-time. Ask you own customers. Read consumers' research. Test competitors. Ask social service leaders whenever you meet.
4. Think long and hard about your "out of hours" service. For instance a 2012 US survey found that of 23 major brands studied, an average of over 4,000 inbound tweets come between 12:00 and 1:00 AM PST.
5. If not running a 24 × 7 operation, use your last tweet of the day to remind customers of "out of hours" alternatives. Make sure these services are operational, allowing customers to leave messages and be informed when their message will be followed up. Put in monitoring to track this traffic.
6. Use your Twitter profile and infobox (left of main profile area) to define your service purpose, the account's authenticity, standard availability, indicative level of responsiveness, out of hours service alternatives, self-help links, language capability, time zone, geographic coverage, other service channels, common service hashtags and security reminders on personal info, e.g. Banks.
7. Use the Lists function to provide useful links such as other Twitter feeds or product links.
8. Cross-promote other service channels using a custom designed background.
9. Consider changing background image as part of crisis response to promote important information.
10. Develop an early warning system to provide maximum time for contingency resourcing.

11. Avoid cut and paste answers. Be as human in your presentation and communication style as possible:

    (a) Both @askciti and @AutodeskHelp provide great examples of profiling the team who are serving you.

    (b) Use initials (with/without circumflex e.g. "^") or first names to sign off and personalize each response. The use of signatures can help customers who wish to tweet a specific person in your team. However, think through continuity policies if adopted.

    (c) "Thank you" remains a powerful phrase.

    (d) Twitter is an easy way to make people feel special – all it takes is 140 characters.

12. Show empathy. Saying "I am sorry" both publicly and privately goes a long way. Your legal team may object to your doing so, but it's critical that you validate the feelings that the customer is having at that moment.

13. Keep the customer informed if the answer is not going to be immediate.

14. One of the keys to great support is to help the most people you can in the shortest amount of time. If you have a very widespread problem with lots of incoming tweets in a short amount of time, using DMs can work. This is the technique:

    (a) Send one public tweet explaining the situation. Anyone who finds your Twitter profile will see that tweet first

    (b) Then reply to any @mentions with a DM. You won't clutter your business's Twitter stream with @replies for other customers looking for what is going on. You can also go into more detail explaining how you can help each customer.

    (c) Switch back to sending @replies once things are fixed.

15. Work with your legal team to codify the scenarios in which advisors still have to refer up-line for guidance. Turn it into a

playbook and train them in it. Empower your team to answer questions quickly with pre-approved content.

16. Invest in regular discussions about communication style to calibrate understanding on what does and does not work for your brand. Find the following examples for case studies:

   (a) In 2012 O2 suffered a number of service outages. Their tweeting style helped get them through.

   (b) A reference to Star Trek by Time Warner Cable did not go down well with Sir Patrick Stewart. Find out what happened.

   (c) Compare Harrods' form of Twitter engagement with Topshop's as examples of differing brand values.

Summary

Ensure your advisors are trained to tweet in the consistent style that you want. It's a very public platform if it goes wrong. A lot of the same common sense Customer Service rules apply. Never get defensive or blame the customer. Instead focus on the solution and be positive and responsive. And while there is often a lot of negativity posted, once you have responded and corrected the issue you may be amazed at the appreciation given back! So what are you waiting for?

Chapter 8

Reputation and Crisis Management

"ACKNOWLEDGE! So much about social customer service is just about your customers being heard. If you acknowledge their posts and tweets you are more than half way there."

Michael Pace, Head of Customer Care and Cultivation,
PerkStreet Financial

So what happens when a disgruntled customer decides to take to social media and berate your brand in full view of the world? Let's start by taking a step back to understand what can trigger this.

People get upset when an organization fails them in a way that matters. A few years ago, *MIT Sloan Management Review* offered a fascinating analysis as to why normally balanced people lose it and start to rant uncontrollably online. They discovered that when organizations significantly fail to honour their side of an agreement made with a customer over a service failure, things get bad. But things go ballistic when it occurs more than twice. At that point there is volcanic eruption from the sense of betrayal. And it takes a long time before that person can be reasoned with again.

This is the extreme of how we can react. Of course there are lesser injustices that can still make us feel the need to attack a brand. To this end it is important to keep a constant look out for your "high influence" customers, celebrities and super users. These are usually those with high numbers of active followers. But be warned, this will not safeguard you. You cannot give "bend-over-backwards" problem resolution to only this profile of customer. You only need read the interview with Dave Carroll of United Breaks Guitars earlier in the book to understand how a previously anonymous customer can cause serious reputational and financial damage.

We also should remember that those in the digital world often rally to each other's aid. Here is a story from 2010 that is extreme in every respect. A woman went to the movies and afterwards wrote a letter to the company complaining about the experience she and her husband and another couple had. She complained that the cinema offered no option to purchase tickets with a credit or debit card. This meant she and her husband had to use their cash for the tickets and then borrow money from the other couple to purchase refreshments. The lobby ATM was reportedly out of cash. Then, she said, the staff interrupted the movie to check the ticket stubs of the seated audience.

Wanting to inflict a little pain for her ruined experience she concluded "I did not pay $18.00 to have a distracted experience. I would rather drive to White Bear Lake, where they obviously know how to run a theatre than have this experience again."

Her barb obviously sunk in and the cinema's vice president made the fatal mistake of doing a "Fawlty Towers".

Sarah,

Drive to White Bear Lake and also go **** yourself. If you don't have money for entertainment, get a better job, and don't pay for everything on your credit or check card. You can also shove your time and gas up your ****ing *ss. Also, find better things to do with your time. This email is an absolute joke. We don't care to have you as a customer. Let me know if you need directions to White Bear Lake

Name Removed – Vice President

That unfortunate outburst led to the immediate creation of a Facebook group called *Boycott St Croix Falls Cinema 8*. In the end, over 4,300 people joined the Facebook group, roughly twice the population of St Croix Falls (which was 2,133 at the 2010 census). Picketing was planned, and heated online discussions took place over several months. The cinema tried to back pedal but it was too little too late. The volcano kept burning.

A further example of how a customer can rally support is illustrated in our interview with Jamie McDonald, where he describes suffering a corporate "mugging" on Carillion's Facebook page. This was "a co-ordinated attack" using friends and family. It was the result of a simple failure to spot one customer's sense of perceived injustice and make good in time.

So what are the lessons here?

> Give customers your attention freely and early on in the process. Respond quickly, even if it is just an early acknowledgement of the issue. The speed of response should ideally be within 15 minutes.

By responding to your customers early on you are doing two things. Firstly, sidestepping a potential reputational crisis for your organization, and secondly letting the rest of the team know that they don't need to rally just yet.

The double-edged sword of Social Customer Service is that it is a public platform which means your highs are high and your lows are low. Everyone can see your response and what you do next will either calm them or incite them. If you start saying "it's policy" or "it's not our issue" or any other defensive, automated, repetitive phrases then you are not helping yourself and you are not helping the customer either.

> Speak to your customers in a natural and upbeat tone. Never argue, blame or get defensive or quote statutory policy. These are sins of Customer Service in any channel but in social it is suicide. Apologize sincerely and reassure.

This is one area that Social Customer Service can learn from contact centres in their use of quality assurance. It is important to monitor the quality of the written communication that is being sent to customers, especially in sensitive situations. Find a way to do this without disempowering the front line or slowing down the response times. This might mean encouraging advisors to check each other's work, or having a coach/floor-walker role in addition to the usual team leader role. The brand needs a consistent tone of voice and advisors need to be applying correct grammar and spelling.

When does a drama become a crisis?

Appeasing an individual customer is one thing. But what's the protocol when something much greater takes place and takes over the whole of your corporate attention and resources? One small problem can become a viral crisis. Especially if it is interesting, emotional or controversial and has a memorable hashtag, it starts to characterize a crisis.

Sometimes issues can bubble away and then fizzle out without you having to do anything. But they can explode. Sometimes this is through your own doing even though the consequences are not clear at the time. Did Tesco anticipate that a pre-scheduled post reading "we're off to hit the hay" would cause such a furore prior to the horsemeat scandal? Suddenly the post was in very bad taste and brought out another lesson for social media crisis management: turn off all your pre-scheduled posts and tweets!

Sometimes things go wrong for uncontrollable reasons such as when BT had to use Twitter to scale their communication and meet customer demand during the 2011 London riots as the emergency 999 service became overwhelmed with calls.

What are some of the core competencies required?

Listening and having the skills to contain the issue with good engagement is always a good first step.

A crisis was experienced by O2 on 11 and 12 July 2012 when the Telecoms brand suffered an embarrassing and lengthy network outage across the UK. The lack of service affected calls, text and data for significant numbers of its own 23 million customers, as well as customers from Tesco Mobile and giffgaff that use O2 masts.

Customers took to social media to vent their frustration and O2 was soon trending on Twitter. The measure of negative sentiment was "anger" and "sadness" in over 2,500 tweets which were then viewed by an estimated 1.7 million people. This is pretty grim for any Social Customer Service team.

But their chirpy conversational tone, use of appropriate humour and humility won the majority of people around. The sentiment barometer swung from "anger" to "love" which reached around half a million people. O2 attracted 13.5 k new Twitter followers as a result and were still engaging with customers when the outage was over, thus further highlighting its resolution. How neat is that?

Whilst the voice of your brand has been something we have repeatedly emphasized for you to be clear and consistent about, it is scrutinized all the more in a crisis situation.

"Know your brand's voice – is it smart and sassy or professional and classical? Be consistent in the style and be sure it fits the brand."
Michael Pace – Head of Customer Care and Cultivation,
PerkStreet Financial

As we mentioned earlier the HMV redundancy drama briefly spilled over into public view. It is worth noting some of the ingredients that turned this drama into a brief crisis for the brand:

1. A memorable hashtag.
2. Emotion (HMV is a long-standing, well-loved UK brand and the shock and horror of what was unfolding was gripping).
3. Controversy (publically hijacking a corporate account).
4. Humour (the reported comment from a panicked Marketing Director asking "how to shut down Twitter" caused much fun subsequently for crisis veterans).

Employees that have been promoting the use of social media in your own company are well positioned to understand how to leverage social media against your organization in a crisis too.

The lesson here is that people who manage social media engagement often don't have a strong enough connection with people at the front. Be careful who at the frontline has access to the social account. Some of the examples of social media flare-ups have started with inexperienced staff members. Equally think about how night staff cover might react. It is easy for inappropriate behaviour to slip out when working in a tired, lonely or emotional state. Choose those people with care.

"Controlling the security of your system is very important. HMV has taught everyone that. Admin registers the twitter account on the admin side and then shares the relevant access to individuals, but those individual users never have the username and password. This gives you more control . . . as long as you trust your admin!"

Leon Chaddock – Managing Director, Sentiment Metrics

One of the best ways to encourage the right behaviour is to have an agreed common approach to assessment. This then allows everyone to be rehearsed in how to act when under pressure. The one we recommend using as a template is the "Air Force Web Posting Response Assessment V.2". It is easily found online. This is a tried and tested approach that many use for managing every day interaction.

Further preparation is needed though to manage crisis level events. Develop a common crisis policy and drill. Get people thinking about "what if" and train them in the policy. Run simulations to discover where the holes are. It often comes down to simple matters. Maybe the right person cannot access something such as the Twitter logon details!

What is your communication capability? Do you proactively contact stakeholders during a crisis across all channels; or do you acknowledge your lack of resources and try to guide all your stakeholders to a single source of company information where you can articulate your position? It is one approach or the other.

Not many companies can afford to have a large number of people "on stand-by" waiting for a crisis to happen. It might be possible to prepare other people from other teams or departments to be ready to help, but will they be needed to help in their own areas? If you are outsourcing your crisis management, check that the people that you anticipate will be handling an "out of hours" crisis will actually be the people that you expect! Not always the case.

In terms of how people work together during a crisis, here is one approach as recommended by Josh Marsh.

> "Get the CEO/Board in a room with the communications and social teams to craft a fast response, allowing the social team to start engaging and responding with customers 1-on-1. Get hourly reports back from the social team back to Comms and the board. Get the responses flowing through that feedback loop."

Having now covered some of the issues, let's look at the best practices you might want to adopt as part of your own pre-planned approach. The following ideas have been distilled from a wide variety of online sources offering their insights, often as a result of lessons learned.

The first list focuses on the key stages with a typical crisis. The second is more concerned with communication etiquette on Facebook and community during a crisis.

Crisis best practice

1. Use the skills of "active listening" throughout. Listen hard. Seek to understand the other person's reality. Don't become personally involved. Ensure communication has succeeded. In fact consider training up key players in the crisis management team. This will help you meet your goal of effective communication which lies at the heart of effective crisis response.
2. Listen before responding. Make sure you really understand the issue and what is driving their emotional response. But be quick.

3. Acknowledge the situation. For an individual customer crisis this may need a reply post on the relevant social channel. For a crisis that affects many customers consider a full acknowledgement on your website linked via social channels.

4. Use the power of saying sorry to help heal relationships. Remember you are not admitting liability by apologizing for the experience. The exact root cause can be determined later. Never imply it might be the customer's fault (even if it could be).

5. As soon as you have confirmation you made an error apologize quickly and sincerely. If you messed up admit that too. Best to be proactive with the truth. And take care to communicate it exactly as you want it received. Trust is lost when others have to fight you for the real situation. The affected individual will think better of you for it and the crowds will not feel the need to rally.

6. Let your customer/customers know what steps you are taking, even if you have no definite resolution as yet. They need evidence that you are at least trying for them.

7. Be sensitive to the timing of communication. There is a natural sense when an update is needed. Either you provide it or someone else will create their own version of what's happening.

8. Don't assume it is over until it really is. Fires can smoulder. Keep tracking via your monitoring platform for further rumblings in communities and forums beyond the obvious large channels and remain ready to respond. This might mean having a trusted and empowered employee(s) ready to proactively respond at any time 24 × 7.

9. Ensure that the person responding is fully trained in necessary guidelines to create and post responses with minimal levels of sign-off. Whilst you can pre-empt some guidelines there also needs to be some autonomy to create customized and individual responses that acknowledge (directly with "@mentions" or Facebook "tags") what the person is saying. Without this the comments from your brand will sound robotic and de-personalized. Too many layers of approval will only slow things down.

10. Be careful about "liking" or replying to supportive comments directed towards your brand in a crisis. Selectively "liking" and rewarding the positive sentiment is potentially going to fuel more negative sentiment. Instead, just "like" and thank the generic posts that don't refer to the crisis detail as you would usually.

11. Remain consistent with your brand voice, don't regress into legalese even if you are being advised by a legal team. Translate it into straightforward language and keep the tone honest, open and blame-free. The communication goal is to come across authentically so those involved stay engaged with you.

12. Ensure that your legal advice is sound. See Chapter 9 for more detail. Make sure as part of your contingency planning that legal expertise is available for certain scenarios.

13. When it is all over, come back together and learn from your crisis handling. Evaluate what worked well and what didn't. Gather data from your monitoring platforms so that you can best focus your efforts in future situations and consider the impact on engagement. As previously mentioned, O2 is a great example of how sentiment can be managed with a well-handled approach.

Facebook and community best practice

1. Be clear about the posting policy of your online community or Facebook pages. Explain why a post might be deleted, edited or hidden (e.g. on Facebook the latter makes it still visible to the post author and their friends but not to your other fans). Never allow a user to be abusive to your staff or other community members. However, do not delete a post just because you don't agree with it or because it is negative towards your brand. Let customers express their dissatisfaction. If you don't they will merely turn up the volume and/or go somewhere else to express it.

2. Use tools and permissions to pick up keywords that could indicate obscenity, abuse or hatred. Block profane language. Don't block the

word "hate" though as this could be used innocuously in everyday speech. Keep revisiting your keywords and adding or evolving them as needed. If your page or community has already been active at this point just be aware that any tools or parameters that you set now won't necessarily go back through posts that have already been submitted. Only new posts will be blocked or "pending approval".

3. If you have a person who keeps attacking in an abusive way on the forums or pages, consider banning or blocking them. It is about facilitating a civil and open discussion without allowing offensive posts. You could consider removing the offensive elements and re-posting if you really want to make a point that you are allowing freedom of speech/expression but in a polite and civil manner. Make sure your re-post explains why you have had to edit and re-post.

4. Keep your ego out of it. Remember the St Croix cinema example. Count to ten, take a step back. You can't please everyone all of the time and it isn't about you personally. It may be painful, but sometimes taking one on the chin is better than getting into a bar fight. Sometimes the more you publicly engage with someone, the more they will use it against you. Simply reply politely that you would be happy to continue the discussion offline and answer any specific questions they may have.

5. Thank people for their feedback and comments. They have taken time to engage with your brand (even if you don't like it much) and as such the information is always useful at some level. Keep focused on the solution. At the end of the day, the solution is the best fix.

Chapter 9

The Legalities of
Social Interaction

Throughout the book we have discussed the voice of social. However, "formal" your core brand might be, we have seen that social communication is often more relaxed and human in style. This is one of its greatest attractions to customers. We've also discussed that in a crisis situation, you have to place significant trust in the front line team to get it right. Often this requires an authentic style of engagement.

All of this however, has to be delivered in an appropriate manner as far the law is concerned. Each territory you operate in has relevant legislation you need to understand and abide by. The social networks you operate in have their own terms and conditions that they expect you to conform to. Making sure that you are fully informed then incorporating this into appropriate policy, training and oversight is a crucial management task. One that also requires frequent updating.

As more legislation is issued, social media strategists will have to strike a careful balance between the culture of compliance and the culture of open communication. In practical terms, make sure that you invest in ongoing discussion with the teams around legal boundaries and consequences so that they understand it but are not intimidated by it.

To provide you with some idea of what to look out for, we asked Katy Howell to talk us through some of the current issues as applied to any use of social media. Katy is CEO of Immediate Future, a social media consultancy with expertise in ensuring a best practice approach to social media and the law. It is clear from her examples that the law is becoming increasingly applied and case histories are emerging from social, involving employees, retweets and copyright.

Please note that this is should not be considered as legally binding advice. Context, territory and other significant factors need to be understood beforehand. Consult experts to provide you with the relevant advice that fits your circumstances.

Copyright infringement, intellectual property theft, libel, defamation and data protection are all part of the business landscape. And that includes social media. But how much do you pay attention to the legal ramifications when engaging in social conversations?

High profile cases such as Wikileaks or the retweeting of allegations against Lord Alistair McAlpine grab the headlines. In the latter case, the consequence was several defamation cases and the possibility of thousands more. In this case it is the retweeter who has to prove the truthfulness of their retweet. Not a situation any organization wants to find itself in.

Social media platforms, such as Facebook, Pinterest, Twitter and YouTube, provide vital tools for business communications. Already a range of statutory media and privacy legislation applies to all company, employee and personal communications. But as social media dominates our everyday lives, so too will the law attempt to impose a legal framework around these networks.

And businesses need to take social seriously. Too many are encouraging branded social profiles to proliferate across social networks with, in many cases, staff posting content with impunity. Ignorance of the law is no longer an excuse for social. District Judge Andrew Shaw made the legal position clear in a high profile footballer case. He outlined that individuals must take responsibility for information and content they share on social networks: ignorance of the law is not a defence. The result was nine criminal convictions and fines. When businesses post on social media, they become publishers. And these publications are subject to the same laws as professional media such as magazines and newspapers. There are consequences to now consider before you tweet, post or upload.

Savvy companies are helping their front line social media communicators understand how the law applies. Coca-Cola, for instance, doesn't allow any of its staff to post a single piece of content on any of its social media networks until they have completed the company's Social Media Certification Program.

Whilst there are a number of high profile brands deploying best practice, the full picture tells a different story. Two-thirds of companies are not very aware of the "Terms of Use" on social platforms. This leaves brands exposed when trying to defend social media actions. When it comes to wider litigations issue, respondents in a recent survey by immediate future didn't feel very informed either. Over 68% of people have basic, beginners or no personal knowledge of social media law.

Having established the risks, how can businesses minimize the threat? For a start, it means implementing the right policies, guidelines, contracts and working practices. Preventing the use of social media in your business will only force the issues underground. It doesn't even necessarily prevent litigation as the company may still be exposed to vicarious liability. Just as importantly, it leaves employees in the dark. They won't appreciate their legal responsibilities when using social networking. It is far more effective and valuable to the business to implement a training and educational programme.

English law does not protect privacy with any specific legislation. However, there is a common law of "right to confidence" that states that with any unauthorized use of published material there is a right to privacy of the material's owners. The law of confidence has been generally applied to intellectual property where a "confidant" has stated they will maintain the confidentiality of the "confider" with regard to any materials they have created.

The test case *Douglas and Others v Hello! Ltd* (2001) is a good example, where Michael Douglas and Catherine Zeta-Jones granted *OK! Magazine* exclusive rights to publish photographs of their wedding. *Hello!* obtained secret photos of the wedding, which the Douglases had not given their permission to publish.

Mr Justice Lindsay found in favour of the claimants in this case awarding the Douglases £7,000 in special damages for costs associated with rearranging the publication of the official photographs. By far the largest award however, went to *OK!* They were awarded damages of just over £1 million. Pay very close attention to the "right of confidence" as failure to do so could be a costly mistake!

When the law of confidence is applied to social media, user-generated content would fall under its remit. Brands that intend to include user-generated content in their campaigns must ensure permission is obtained. Brands should pay specific attention when using real names and other personal information from user-generated content. Otherwise the owner of these materials could claim that their privacy and the "contract of confidence" have been broken. Moreover, if a personal loss can be proven as a consequence of the alleged breach of confidence, the awards of damages can be high.

As we increasingly see the application of the "right of confidence" to social media, there are a number of important existing pieces of legislation that are also being applied to social media activity. These include data protection, privacy and defamation. There is established case and statutory law in the areas of intellectual property protection and privacy.

It is important to be aware of these, and know when to request specialist advice from a legal team or firm. The onus is on the business to be aware of relevant legislation and keep up to date, especially if you are to fully appreciate how these apply to the social networks used for business. In many cases there is an absence of law specifically developed for social networks. Therefore, businesses must assume that existing legislation applies to all social activities.

Privacy, copyright and data protection are your responsibility

Your customers, consumers and stakeholders are uploading and posting increasing quantities of personal information online. Some of this information they will share with your company. You might have asked for user-generated content, contact details or email addresses. It is the business's responsibility to ensure this information is fully protected – if you are to avoid costly legal battles under the Data Protection Act 1998 and the Data Protection Regulations 2014.

The basic principles of the Data Protection Act impact on social media activity. By the very nature of developing close one-to-one relationships with your audiences, various departments will often collect, store and otherwise manipulate information and are therefore bound by the Act to protect the personal data that they are using. Data must be:

- Processed legally and fairly
- Processed only for a limited purpose
- Relevant and sufficient for the purpose the data is being used for
- Collected, stored and used accurately
- Kept only for as long as is necessary
- Processed in accordance with the rights of the individual
- Only transferred to other countries that have comparable data protection controls.

How long you store the data matters too. Don't keep personal data culled from social media networks for longer then you need to, as this is a basic principle of the Data Protection Act 1998.

The EU Justice Commission is looking to reform the legal framework around data protection. The new regulations are expected to wrap around the existing Data Protection Directive from 1995, and fix the new regulations in law. There will be a strong focus on privacy across all EU Member States by 2014. When the new legislation comes into force, the plan is that the EU will have just one enforcement authority. One that both businesses and consumers can use as a point of contact for data protection and information privacy. The Commission says the exercise would save industry €2.3 billion (US$3 billion) annually.

The new EU regulations are likely to influence how organizations develop social media initiatives. Ensuring full compliance with the existing Data Protection Act in the UK will, in the future, be joined by the new EU regulations, although there is some debate as to when and how the UK will adopt the legislation. If the EU changes are adopted in the UK, it is likely to mean businesses will have more responsibility for the data they collect and use.

It is important to view your business's Twitter and Facebook profiles, YouTube or Pinterest channels and the blogs and forums that your business uses as extensions of your company. No one is claiming that the law as it stands at the moment was designed for social media networks, but legal practitioners are warning their clients to be on their guard.

Copying of images and other materials was rife in the early days of the internet, and today images are still frequently used without the permission of the owner. Copyright is a core component of intellectual property (IP) law. It has been under the spotlight since the inception of the internet. But these days businesses must pay much closer attention to the copyright protection of their own work, and how their organization uses other materials in their promotional activity and, of course, across their social media profiles.

The Copyright, Designs and Patents Act 1988 is the core piece of legislation that must be adhered to in the UK. But copyright has regional focus. There are no universal and international laws of copyright, as each country has their own. As many of the social networks your business is using are based in the US, it is important to pay attention to UK *and* US copyright regulations to avoid any possible infringement litigation.

It is also important to understand the relationship that social networking sites have with the content that they distribute. A social media network like Facebook acts as a connector and does not own or enforce any copyright of the content owners. You are not able to sue the social media network for any alleged infringement of copyright; it is the responsibility of your business to police this. You need to know the "Terms of use" for every social media platform that you use. Upon signing up to create an account with a channel you will accept the terms in their entirety. Visit the sites for the latest terms and conditions of use. Currently 66% of social media professionals are not aware of the T&Cs on individual networking sites like Facebook and Twitter.

Many companies are keen to foster greater engagement with stakeholders. One way is to encourage the sharing of user-generated content.

And this technique can really help foster dialogue and deepen relationships with the brand. Indeed, a campaign for the Ford Fiesta only uses materials created by its brand advocates in social media and on review websites.

However, it is the organization's responsibility to protect the interests and confidentiality of customers when using copyrightable materials. And don't forget that the materials that are used should be preserved in an accessible format, to protect your business in the event of a copyright infringement claim. In a recent survey 46% of Marketers questioned were not aware of the intellectual property rights associated with user-generated content.

There are tools that can back up *all* your social media channels regularly, in a way that is local to you (not on the servers of a third party). If you can combine both your backup/archive requirements with a tool that helps monitor engagement all the better – SocialSafe is one such tool.

With the advent of the internet and the ease with which content could be copied, copyright legislation and the protection it afforded was clearly lacking. Image copyright infringement and theft was rife in the early days of the internet. The Web is still awash with images that can be copied with just a right-click of your mouse. But today as originators and owners of content have realized the commercial value of their images, they are becoming more litigious when it comes to alleged infringements of their images.

Copyright protection has attempted to keep up with the changes in technology.

Out of the copyright vacuum grew Creative Commons. This non-profit organization was founded to offer an alternative set of copyright licences. One where originators could control how their work is distributed. Creators can decide how much of their intellectual property they reserve and how much they waive. This flexibility is a significant shift in how copyright has been viewed in the past, when there was an inflexible "all rights reserved" licence attached to *all* copyrightable works.

Who owns the content on social media profiles?

The laws of copyright are clear: once the expression of an idea is in a tangible form (images, text, audio and video) copyright regulations apply, which extend to the life of the creator plus 70 years.

Social media profiles that your business sets up need to be considered with care. Especially when thinking about who owns the social profile – you, your employee or a freelance support? The case of *Phonedog v Kravitz* is a good example.

Here Phonedog hired Noah Kravitz to help with their Twitter account. He set up an account in the name of @Phonedog_Noah which went on to attract 17,000 followers. When Kravitz left the company Phonedog wanted the Twitter account reverted back to them. However, Kravitz simply changed the account name to @NoahKravitz and continued to use the account. The case was finally settled late in 2012, with Kravitz maintaining control of the Twitter account.

> "If anything good has come of this, I hope it's that other employers and employees can recognize the importance of social media . . . good contracts and specific work agreements are important, and the responsibility for constructing them lies with both parties."
>
> Noah Kravitz

There is a further grey area to consider. Who owns your business social media profiles? Some employees are now active across the social networks on behalf of their employers. Many will build, in some cases, highly detailed profiles with information and contact lists that could have a high commercial value. It is important that businesses build unambiguous statements regarding the ownership of these profiles and the data they contain into their contracts of employment. It is even more important that they make this clear from the outset of any social activity.

Clearly, there must be a balance between businesses wanting their employees to become active social media users and businesses wanting to also protect themselves and ensure that ownership of the data created resides with the business.

The case of Mark Lons is a good example. He was ordered by the High Court to return the list of contacts he had built up on the LinkedIn social network whilst working for Hays, which he used to set up his own consultancy business. Hays claimed that Lons had broken the terms of his employment contract. Lons attempted to counterclaim that the information on his LinkedIn account was in the public domain. However, Justice Richards disagreed, ordering Lons to hand over all materials linked to the contacts on his LinkedIn account.

1. Has your business ensured that you have the rights and permissions to use "user-generated content"?
2. Have assets such as images, videos and audio files been cleared for use by their respective copyright holders for use online and within social media specifically?
3. Have all trademarks been acknowledged on all marketing collateral and attributions made where required under creative commons?
4. Have all employees been briefed about what materials they can and can't use on their social media postings?
5. Has all social media marketing collateral been fully protected with contracts that stipulate how these materials can and can't be used?
6. Has a clear path of escalation been established if alleged copyright infringement is made against your company?

Retweet recourse

The ease with which a tweet can be written and posted can be a major headache for businesses that are trying to control how this platform is being used by their staff.

Consider the case of former New Zealand cricket captain Chris Cairns. He won a defamation case against Lalit Modi. The award totalled £90,000 – that works out at £3,750 per word tweeted!

The Defamation Act 1996 does provide that: "In defamation proceedings a person has a defence if he shows that: (a) he was not the author, editor or publisher of the statement complained of, (b) he took reasonable care in relation to its publication, and (c) he did not know, and had no reason to believe, that what he did caused or contributed to the publication of a defamatory statement."

Here ignorance of the alleged defamatory statement could be successful as this is a provision of the Act. Brands should not rely on this though, and check the accuracy of all statements.

Tweets have a number of pieces of legislation that could impact on any given message. Businesses must pay particular attention to the law of defamation. It isn't just original tweets. Part of your content strategy will be to curate content; and that means sharing other people's posts. It is very tempting to retweet a post (and so quick to do). The retweeting of alleged paedophile names by thousands of people – including celebrities – has shown that retweeting information without legal checks can lead to litigation. And some pretty hefty fines!

Before a tweet is sent or retweeted, you need to consider whether the tweet reduces a person's standing in society in "the estimation of right-thinking members of society". If it does, there could be a case for libel.

Menacing and malicious tweets also fall under the law. Here, the law makes it clear that harassment has taken place: "if a reasonable person in possession of the same information would think the course of conduct amounted to or involved harassment".

Also, a tweet that is proven to be grossly offensive could fall under the Communications Act 2003, which states that satirical comments are allowed, but tweets that are obscene could fall under the Act. But the law can be grey sometimes, as shown by the example of Paul Chambers which demonstrates the issue. In a fit of frustration he tweeted: "Crap! Robin Hood airport is closed. You've got a week and a bit to get your shit together otherwise I'm blowing the airport sky high!!" The court immediately applied existing laws. But on appeal there was a rethink on how legislation like the Communications Act actually applies to social media.

The High Court ruling – that was subsequently overturned – stated:

The potential recipients of the message were the public as a whole, consisting of all sections of society. It is immaterial that [Chambers] may have intended only that his message should be read by a limited class of people, that is, his followers, who, knowing him, would be neither fearful nor apprehensive when they read it.

In our judgment, whether one reads the "tweet" at a time when it was read as "content" rather than "message", at the time when it was posted it was indeed "a message" sent by an electronic communications service for the purposes of [the Communications Act], Accordingly "Twitter" falls within its ambit.

Companies must pay close attention to the content of tweets when they describe a product or a service. False statements about a product's features, for instance, could result in a claim by a customer that they bought the goods based on the information contained within a tweet that then proved to be false.

Whilst it is tempting to copy the content of tweets and pass this off as an original post, this should be avoided. This kind of activity could fall foul of the Copyright, Designs and Patents Act 1988. Isolated sentences may be used, as this could constitute "fair use" which is allowed under the Act. However, new directives from the European Court of Justice may mean that more attention will have to be paid to how the alleged copied materials were then used in a new tweet. And the use of the hashtag in association with a trademark should be carefully considered. Using the hashtag with another company's trademarked name could result in a claim of infringement depending on how the hashtag was used within the tweet. No business wants a claim made against them under The Trade Marks Act 1994.

The use of images that originally appeared on social media sites such as Twitter should also be approached with caution. Images of breaking news stories that are quickly picked up by all the major news agencies illustrate the speed with which images can be reused without the proper checks on copyright ownership.

Twitter is the only organization to have the right to use their images as stated in their terms and conditions. For everyone else, proper copyright clearance should have been obtained.

Twitter is now more proactive when alleged copyright infringements are reported to them.

They will provide details of the complaint and also information about how a counter-claim can be made. This is an interesting shift in the stance of social networks that have, until now, taken the view that they are simply a hosting platform for their users' content. Whether the other major social media networks will follow suit and become more involved with copyright complaints remains to be seen.

1. Do think about why a tweet being is sent. Make sure that content is always in support of a well-defined campaign or service guidelines.
2. Do ensure all members of staff have full knowledge of your company's policy regarding content sent via Twitter.
3. Do make sure all tweets, or content that could be defined as offensive, are vetted for copyright materials. A checklist for your community manager is a useful way to ensure that all the elements are remembered.
4. Do carefully consider your use of a hashtag that is used by a competitor or other business or product as trademark infringement could result.
5. Do check retweeted content for its legality and take the time to verify any claims.
6. Do ensure your company's security policy includes Twitter and how this should be used. And keep it up to date.

Mixing staff and social

Increasingly, businesses are realizing that Human Resources must also take care when using social media networks in their activities. The use of social media profiles as a tool for recruitment is growing rapidly. Companies are also monitoring social profiles of their employees too.

It is vital that HR, marketing and PR departments integrate their efforts when using social media to avoid potential litigation. The demarcation lines between posting comments on social media networks as an individual and as an employee are blurry at best when it comes to case law.

The right to privacy?

In the case of *Teggart v TeleTech UK Ltd*, an employee was dismissed for posting offensive comments on his Facebook page. When the case came to tribunal it was ruled that as he had placed his comments on a publicly accessible site he could, therefore, not rely on his right to privacy and a private life under the Human Rights Act. His comments were defined as harassment with his claim for unfair dismissal being rejected by the tribunal.

The use of social media networks by employees has been a contentious issue, but one that HR departments have to manage. Employment law had not envisaged a communications channel that could be used by employees to reach the customers of their employers in such an intimate way. However, case law such as *Seaman & Cooke* (2010) has shown that employees who make false statements – in this case on their Facebook page – can find the post to be deemed defamatory because of the inaccurate nature of the comments made.

What has become clear is that HRs need to develop a tailored social media policy that clearly sets out what is appropriate content for the social networks used by their employees. A clear example is the Joe Gordon case. Gordon was dismissed as an employee of Waterstones for writing inappropriate content about his employer on his blog. Following a disciplinary hearing, Gordon was originally dismissed. But he successfully challenged in an appeal, supported by some high profile media coverage. Waterstones should have had clear guidelines and a policy in place to avoid not only a court case, but reputational damage created by the widespread media coverage.

The social media usage policy of all companies needs to be written with a view to balance. Businesses understand that there is a commercial component to social media they can't ignore, but limits have to be placed on employees to reduce the potential for damaging comments. However, the laws that protect whistleblowing ("protected disclosure") must be protected to ensure that your social media policy doesn't infringe this right that all employees have.

For HRs social media is somewhat of an unknown entity. Until we have enough case law, and also tests via employment tribunals, all that HRs can do on a practical level is ensure that their employee policies are clear about what is allowed when social media networks are considered, and take into consideration existing legislation that impacts on privacy, intellectual property and libel.

To protect themselves employers should:

1. Ensure that employee handbooks include detailed guidance on what their company expects when social media networks are used.
2. Managers should be equipped with training to ensure that staff under their supervision can be properly educated about the accepted use of social media sites.
3. Employers can monitor access and use of social media networks by their employees, but this must be clearly stated – and agreed to – by employees in their employment contract.
4. Any postings that are made to social media sites should be clearly marked as either personal views of the employee, or that their comments are sanctioned by their employers and reflect the company view.

Your Social Media Policy

Employee social networking activity can have a huge impact on every business. It is vital that a policy document is developed that concisely sets out what your business expects from everyone using social media.

Today it's not viable to ban the use of social media networks. It cannot be controlled either in work (because of mobile access) or outside of working hours. A social media policy can ensure that everyone in your company understands how to use these networks to minimize the legal risks they pose.

However, a social media policy shouldn't be a dusty document left on a shelf or buried in the employee handbook. Keep it direct, concise and interesting – it should aim to engage and be relevant to your employees.

What should a social media policy include?

1. Before you even begin, "social media" should be defined. Your policy should make it clear that any site that is within the social media sector is covered by your policy, not just the social media networks that are mentioned by name.
2. Ensure your policy is very clear and that it covers both inside and outside of traditional working hours – social media is 24/7 and your policy should reflect that.
3. Inform employees if your business intends to monitor their usage of social media networks and that access can be withdrawn if misuse is identified.
4. You should lay out how your employees can talk about your business, products, customers or clients online. It should be clear

that the material your employees are posting reflects their own views rather than those of the company.

5. Reiterate how your employees should treat both their colleagues and other people on the internet. What they post should not be obscene, defamatory, profane, libellous, threatening, harassing, sexist, racist, prejudiced, abusive, hateful or embarrassing to any other person or entity.

6. Take your draft policy to your legal team and ensure that it is compliant and as watertight as possible. But do also make sure that it is readable and employee friendly.

7. Remind employees that copyright applies to all their social media activity.

8. Emphasize the importance of ensuring the correct level of privacy settings on personal accounts and that employees should understand social networks' terms and conditions before setting up an account.

9. Ultimately, your social media policy should be designed around your business. There is no set template to a social media policy and you have to consider how you want your employees to use social media.

Remember, social media keeps changing. Not just the technology, but customer behaviour changes. Sometimes, very quickly. Your social media policy should be regularly reviewed and updated to include these changes. The best way to manage this is to create a cross-functional working group of senior people. Issues and changes can be discussed as well as programmes and communications refreshed. Better still, feedback and revisions to the policy will keep it fresh and relevant.

Chapter 10

One Agenda: PR, Marketing and Customer Service Working Together

Coming to the end of our exploration around Social Customer Service provides an opportunity to loosen our focus and put the whole discussion into a broader organizational context. In Chapter 2 we talked about the current transformation that "digitalization" is causing. Our personal and professional worlds are being redefined. Social Customer Service is a symptom of the new behaviours being generated.

As far as the world of organizations is concerned, commentators have used various terms such as Enterprise 2.0 and Social Business to label the impact that this transformation is having on the way we work, relate and generate value. Tremendous energy is being invested in bringing this about. And guess what? Two of the most popular sandboxes that house these experiments are internal collaboration amongst employees and external collaboration with customers: both leveraging the dynamic of being social, transparent and real-time.

However, this trend towards collaboration is fighting over a hundred years of corporate habit and history. Long-standing corporate cultures are cemented in place. Their functional structures deeply embedded into the foundations of organizational behaviour. Put more simply, it's going to take a while!

> "Organizations can be really selfish, designing processes for their benefit and not their customers. Many organizations are guilty of making the customer fit with their processes. Then, because there is so much embedded investment in these processes and systems, they keep building on them trying to improve them."
>
> Adrian Swinscoe – consultant, corporate coach and blogger

That is why the whole topic of this book is such an exciting world to be in right now because it is where the old world and new world are colliding. From that exchange of often conflicting priorities are emerging new ways of working and new mindsets.

How that actually happens can be an invisible shift. As Cormac Connolly, Director of Channel Development at Virgin Media, reflected in his interview with us:

"We have got to a really healthy balance across customer care, marketing and PR. Looking back, I would say we got there without making that a deliberate goal, rather an engaging approach and that's the way it played out."

This is a great observation and is one we increasingly hear from the front runners. But what are the issues for those still wading through the treacle? Obviously Sales, Marketing and Service are major organizational touch points for customers. The level and quality of customer experience is largely determined through their actions. Yet most organizations still allow these competencies to operate in silos. This makes them blind to opportunity and ignorant of their combined impact which is one of the reasons why customers seek out social channels to make themselves heard.

If you are a small organization or a very tightly integrated one, then maybe the walls between Sales, Marketing and Service remain semi per-

meable. That necessary co-operation amongst those teams is still facilitated. However, as a rule of thumb, the larger an organization gets, the
more it relies on organization structure to scale.

With that approach comes the seeding and generation of petty king-
doms. And before long, the sense of belonging to a company is only
what's printed on a business card. Instead, the individual experience is of
pledging allegiance first to function, then to brand because that is where
the dynamics of personal careers are played out.

One of the effects of a hundred years of fencing off internal teams is
that there are now different tribes in each of the main customer facing
functions. And tribes suggest unique cultures. Then layered on top of this
natural instinct to see things differently and prioritize accordingly, are the
carrot and stick of siloed organizational targets and incentives.

> "One agenda is fundamental to business success but is practically hard
> for Corporates to enact or work to. The reason I think this is so difficult
> is because they tend to be ruled by KPIs and KPIs tend to be radically
> different from one business function to the next."
>
> Bian Salins – Head of Social in the TV and Media industry.
> Previously Head of Social for a Telcoms company

Add all this together and it is no surprise that "alignment", a sense of
"being on the same team", a "readiness to collaborate" are not front of
mind intentions within these functions. Even when their diplomatic rep-
resentatives meet at executive level, it is often like national ministers
mingling at an EU session!

If you want further proof ask the head hunters. What do they look for
in a sales person, a Marketer or a great Customer Service person? They

know candidates for these roles are quite different in competencies, aspiration, values; even dress code!

Further down the line, we might find this way of working quite strange. For instance, instead of three functional areas there might be just one. Let's call it the Customer Team. Everyone who joins is inducted into the primary disciplines of Sales, Marketing and Service (now holistically joined at the hip). Thereafter each can specialize or remain a generalist. Either way, the team sees everything in the context of customer lifecycle and engagement.

So our point is this. While the big wheel turns and we wait for the blueprint of digital organizational life to arrive we can try and speed things up. And so, unless you are blessed with pre-existing tendencies for front line collaboration, you might appreciate some of these tactics to catalyze a smarter level of customer engagement between functions.

Why One Agenda?

As customers have changed, so too have the demands on front line functions. Increasingly customers are proving themselves able to complete pre and post purchase tasks without their help. Given that, can we continue to work in silos with all the inherent inefficiencies and blind spots this creates? The answer has to be no. So a new mission needs to emerge around a much more closely orchestrated approach to customer engagement.

And this is where the notion of "One Agenda" comes in. It is a milestone. Someway down the line of convergence. It is rooted in a simple observation that the best way to get different tribes to work together is to unify their focus under a common agenda. It also has the virtue of being an easy idea to get across and get busy with. Here are some suggestions to get your own version of One Agenda up and running.

All the following suggestions are intended to prevent further duplication of effort between front line teams. Thereafter, begin an ongoing process of spotting opportunities to pool resources and co-ordinate activity. These initiatives are not initially assumed to be substitutes for existing functional plans. That level of co-operation would probably take at least 12 months to reach in most SMEs and possibly twice as long in enterprise sized organizations. Instead this is all about taking giant sized baby steps.

1. Develop a common view of customers

Each function is likely to have their preferred way of categorizing customers. For instance, how do marketing segments fit with sale funnel categories? These are two very different ways of describing the same customer for different purposes. Can they be linked in any meaningful way? Customer service has its own language as well in term of where customers sit as "open" or "closed" cases.

The first thing to do is getting the teams to recognize this difference and re-examine why they used to label in those ways. Secondly, in the light of changed customer behaviours what is a more relevant taxonomy for a common goal around customer engagement? For instance:

- Valuable customers
- Customers at risk
- Customers with high levels of relevant influence
- Brand advocates.

Another topic well worth discussing is how customer experience is mapped and tracked by each function. Sometimes the customer journey or lifecycle will have been defined: maybe at the level of the key moments of truth. What would happen if everything was pooled and turned into a single, commonly understood version? Suddenly we have a language that can be shared between teams with descriptions of the overall customer state that everyone can use and start tracking.

There is some evidence of this type of collaboration. For instance, AT&T hold a weekly digital leadership council, attended by staff members across e-commerce, customer care, PR & marketing. This helps to ensure that there is clear collaboration between different departments and that everyone responsible for representing the company both offline and online is communicating the same messages.

2. Do joint business planning and projects

One of the root causes of the disconnection between front line functions is the business planning process. Budgets and targets are typically handed down centrally. Yet commentary is then written to support their realization in isolation. This can result in absurdities. Marketing achieves lead generation targets while the Sales team fall short of theirs. Equally Customer Service can suffer the consequences of over inflated marketing messages and over promising Sales people. We have described this train crash on Facebook home pages earlier in the book. So here is a simple set of suggestions to augment the annual planning process.

Teams get together in order to share their own plans and see where they overlap, where they can be synergized and even when new joint aims can be created. For instance, not so long ago a brand's marketing strategy revolved around pushing products at customers. A more joined up approach would encourage organizations to market *with* their customers instead of *to* them, by providing beneficial information, responding to questions and feedback, and interacting on a more personalized level for the reward of brand loyalty. This is how Marketing and Service can merge their interests around a common agenda.

Here is another example of cross-functional teamwork in order to better understand how a unified approach to customer lifecycle management could result in greater customer profitability.

"We found that people who we interacted with socially were more likely to subscribe than people who had emailed in. If someone had over 500 followers and we got a retweet then we knew that someone, somewhere would subscribe out of that."

Maria McCann – Group Head of Customer Experience and Service for Aurora Fashions. Previously headed up Social Customer Service at Spotify and ASOS

What else can be done? It might make sense to generate joint dash-boards to give some form of common insight into the state of the customer experience. NPS has been very successful in becoming a universally understood metric. Are others needed, maybe more suited to the era of social interaction such as the Gratitude Index?

Beyond dashboards, let's think about other ways to shake things up. What about inviting "outsiders" into functional progress meetings and brainstorm sessions. Traditionally these always run the risk of staying within tramlines and working from a set agenda. Fresh eyes from another customer facing department should bring fresh thinking and thus innova-tion. Expand the agendas, think more broadly. Learn about the practical issues facing others related teams. Best way to understand another culture is to visit!

"The Marketing and Customer Service worlds are getting a lot closer. Don't think of vertical silos but as a horizontal customer attraction and retention approach. Communicate with each other and join-up on any promotions and the content management. If customer service spots a moment of opportunity they need to be empowered to use it without asking layers of people."

Michael Pace – Head of Customer Care and Cultivation, PerkStreet Financial

3. Merge customer analytics

This is a slightly tougher assignment than the previous two in so far as analytic solutions are scoped by outside vendors. But just being aware of the opportunity and sharing each other's outputs can go a long way to generating a set of common insights and action points.

For instance, pooling Marketing and Sales analytics should produce a better view of what does and does not work in terms of finding and winning customers. Equally speech analytics could be compared with social analytics to see how customer behaviour aligns or changes across different channels. Moreover a jointly owned and resourced improvement plan, a key output of analytics, is always more likely to succeed when universally backed.

Final thoughts

The value of One Agenda is to help front line teams work together and jointly evolve their competency engaging customers in relevant ways. Social interaction puts greater urgency on getting it right. One Agenda is a challenging but achievable milestone in a much larger journey towards what some are calling the "Social Enterprise". One you might already know as the "Customer Company".

ENDING OR BEGINNING?

Thank you for reading this book; hopefully in its entirety. However, you have consumed it, we wish the very best for your plans. Our aim has been to provide you with a thorough exploration of the Social Customer Service ecosystem and also challenge you to greater achievements wherever you currently sit on that journey.

Neither of us see this book as an ending. We would love to transform what has been a monologue into dialogue. Your feedback, questions and involvement of any kind are really welcome. As we said in the Foreword, we have provided a simple online forum for discussion and sharing of the research materials that helped us write this. If that is not your style a simple email would be great.

Till then go well.

INDEX